GANGES CANAL

GANGES CANAL

A

DISQUISITION

ON THE HEADS OF THE GANGES AND JUMNA CANALS,

NORTH-WESTERN PROVINCES,

IN REPLY TO STRICTURES

MAJOR-GENERAL SIR ARTHUR COTTON

COL. SIR PROBY T. CAUTLEY, K.C.B.

GYAN

Published by

Gyan Publishing House
5, Ansari Road
Daryaganj, New Delhi-110002
Phone: 011-47034999, 9811692060
E-mail: books@gyanbooks.com

Distribution Network
gyanbooks.com
India, USA, Canada, UK, Australia, France

ISBN : 978-81-212-9626-7 (PB)
First Published, 1864

2nd Impression 2023

Printed at: Gyan Press, Delhi.

GANGES CANAL
Author: COL. SIR PROBY T. CAUTLEY, K.C.B.

GANGES CANAL.

A

DISQUISITION

ON THE HEADS OF THE GANGES AND JUMNA

CANALS,

NORTH-WESTERN PROVINCES,

IN REPLY TO STRICTURES

BY MAJOR-GENERAL SIR ARTHUR COTTON.

BY

COL. SIR PROBY T.[Y] CAUTLEY, K.C.B.

1864.

PREFATORY NOTE.

The main point at issue, discussed in this essay, is whether, as an engineering project, the head of the Ganges Canal should have been led off *above* the commencement of the high land of the Northern Doab, where the river runs upon shingle on a high incline; or *below* it, by the construction of a dam across the river, where it flows in a depressed trough, upon a sandy bed. The former plan was adopted by me, and although it has been assailed by Sir Arthur Cotton, I hold that it was the only sound one. But in order to justify it, I have been compelled to enter into minute and tedious details regarding the surface contour of the country; the slopes of the river beds in relation to the higher levels and slope of the land; and the lines of drainage, by which the Doab is longitudinally intersected. These are devoid of interest to the general reader, but they are essential to my explanation. This should be borne in mind, in judging of the space which the *k'hadirs,* river-courses, shingle beds, &c., occupy in the following pages.

It was my earnest wish to avoid a personal controversy with Sir Arthur Cotton: that is clearly shown by the manner in which I met his strictures in my "Reply to Statements." I had determined to close my share in the discussion with that reply (*see* p. 41.) But General Cotton's persevering charge against me of having expended three quarters of a million sterling on works, which he describes as so unnecessary that he could have gained the same object by an outlay of 75,000*l.*; the pertinacity with which he repeats disproved statements; and the idle calumny with which he visits the staff of engineer officers employed upon the Canal establishments in the North Western Provinces, have forced me, reluctantly, to inquire what reliance can be put on his statements and estimates, and whether Sir Arthur Cotton is not better qualified to magnify the mistakes of others, than to be trusted with a project of his own.

London, April 17, 1864.

CONTENTS.

LIST OF PLATES.

A

DISQUISITION

ON THE HEADS OF THE GANGES AND JUMNA CANALS,

ETC. ETC. ETC.

I PROPOSE in the following pages to enter in some detail, on the Jumna and Ganges rivers, as connected with the irrigation canals in the North-Western Provinces —more especially on the measures which have been adopted of drawing a supply for their maintenance; and to explain why, in defiance of the difficulties encountered in contending with mountain torrents, this supply has been taken, both by ancient and modern engineers, from the higher regions where the beds of the rivers consist of boulders and shingle situated on heavy slopes; and why, by avoiding the difficulties above-mentioned, the canal heads have not been placed at points lower down the course of the rivers, where the slopes are less, and where the beds of the rivers consist entirely of sand.

It would appear that in Southern India the latter course is adopted—that is to say, a dam, or anicut[1] (as it is called in the Madras Presidency), the waste-board of which is considerably elevated, is carried across

[1] Anekattu, corruptly Anicut.—*H. H. Wilson's Glossary.*

the bed of the river. The surface of the water is raised so as to enter the canal head, the flooring of which is placed on the same level as the waste-board of the anicut. An artificial reservoir of supply is thus obtained, in lieu of the natural flow of water into the heads which is gained by the establishment of spurs and bunds of shingle on the higher levels of the rivers, as is practised on the canals of the North-West Provinces.

The systems are wholly different. The Madras engineers attack the river in its full volume, and force it to give a supply by an artificial elevation of the water. Those of the North-West studiously avoid the river in its might, and endeavour to escape from artificial elevation by proceeding to the higher levels, and taking advantage of the natural fall of country. In other words, the Madras engineers select the *foot* of a rapid, whilst those of the North-West prefer the *head* as the source whence their canal supply is to be taken.

The plan here described as appertaining to the North-West has been in use from the earlier days of canal making by the old Pathan conquerors; that in Southern India may be traced back to a far earlier period; it has been extended with great effect by Sir A. Cotton, who may be considered the active apostle of the system, and who by his anicuts on the Godaveri and other rivers of the Madras Presidency within the Deltaic segment of their course, has done more for the irrigation of that Presidency than any of his predecessors. The physical conditions, however, of the river systems in the two cases are, in some important respects, widely different, as will be shown in the sequel. That which is suited to the one is not equally applicable to the other.

It is from a discussion that has arisen between Sir Arthur Cotton and myself, in which my plan of adopting the course of those who have preceded me has been severely condemned by Sir Arthur Cotton, that it appears desirable to enter upon the subject more in detail than has as yet been done; more especially as Sir Arthur Cotton complains that neither in my Ganges Canal report, nor in any document referring to projects for the Ganges or Jumna, has he been able to find any discussion on the subject. That the subject has been fully considered and discussed on many occasions during my long connection with the Canal Department, and especially as bearing on the Ganges Canal works, there can be no doubt; but the views and experience of all, whether engineers or civil functionaries of the district, have been so decidedly opposed to interference with the great perennial rivers in their course at the foot of the rapids after they leave the boulders and shingle, and enter the deep alluvial troughs, and my own views are, and have been, so perfectly in accordance with them, that I did not consider it necessary to extend a report which must necessarily be a very long one, on a subject which there appeared to be no object in discussing.

The question, however, involves points beyond those of mere engineering, and they will be treated by me in the following order:—

1st. Engineering difficulties of, and financial objections to, making and maintaining permanent dams across the sandy beds and k'hadir[1] of the Jumna and Ganges.

2nd. Effects upon villages and valuable lands by back-water and inundation caused by the dams.

3rd. Evils, in a sanitary point of view, of creating lakes and morasses with reed and forest jungle, by back-water and inundation.

To these I shall advert hereafter, but my object in the first instance is to bring under review the Jumna

[1] Khadar, or Khadŭr, incorrectly Khadir.—*Wilson's Glossary.* K'hadir.—*Elliot.*

and Ganges rivers themselves, with their topographical features, as connected with the high lands through which they take their course. I do this for the information of those especially who may not have the means of referring to my Ganges Canal report.

Ganges and Jumna Rivers in Connection with the Highlands.—The Ganges and Jumna, after traversing the Himalayas along a course of 165 and 110 miles respectively, open out upon the valley of Deyra. At the points where they leave the Great Himalayan chain, they are separated (measuring from the Jumna at Kuttur Puttur to the Ganges at Rikekhes) by a distance of 38 miles; the Ganges forming the eastern and the Jumna the western boundary of the valley. In their onward progress these two great rivers force a passage through the Sewaliks, a range of tertiary hills that separate the valley from the plains of India. The debouch of the Ganges upon these plains takes place at the town of Hurdwar situated in 29° 58′ N. latitude, whilst that of the Jumna is just below the valley of Kulesur on the right, and the Kharra head of an old branch on the left of the river, in latitude 30° 21′.

Down to this point the Ganges, after leaving the main chain of the Himalayas, leads off the drainage of the eastern slope of the Deyra Valley, through the medium of the combined streams of the Song and Sooswa, as well as that on its left bank through various channels of a subordinate character. The Jumna, in its passage from the Himalayas, has been augmented by drainage, but of much greater importance, as in addition to that of the western slope of the Deyra Valley, carried to it by the Asun river, it has drained on its right bank very extensive tracts of mountain and valley by the Tonse and Girri, two rivers which rise in the Sirmoor country, are perennial in their supply, and bring down in the rains large volumes of water, whilst during the dry months the streams are by no means inconsiderable.[1]

At the town of Hurdwar, and at the Kharra Head, where the Ganges and Jumna leave the mountains and issue into the plains, the dry weather discharge may be estimated at 8,000 and 4,000 cubic feet per second respectively; in seasons of extraordinary drought, this has been diminished, but as a fair average of the amount of discharge during ordinary dry seasons, the above may be accepted with every confidence in its trustworthiness.

The slopes of the beds of the rivers down to the point at which we have arrived is exceedingly great, passing over rock and boulders. In the latter part of their course, after having left the great mountains, they appear in lines of open stream and heavy rapid alternately, some of these rapids being of the most formidable character, one especially on the Jumna in its passage through the Sewaliks called the Dholra Rapid, which, by being directed upon a huge and lofty cliff of sandstone on the left of the river, has become the grave of many a raft and many a raftsman. During the rainy months, this quiet aspect of alternating reaches and rapids is converted into a consecutive mass of rolling water, the rapids being engulfed, and the whole river having the appearance of an overwhelming cataract. The water, during the dry months, and when undisturbed by floods, is as clear as

[1] The Tonse and Girri, in their passage through the mountains, pass through regions of shale, or a fragmentary slate; that which is traversed by the Tonse being black, that by the Girri being deep red. Heavy falls of rain, which locally affect these valleys, are marked by the colour of the water as it pours into the Jumna. I have seen the Girri enter the Jumna River at a point opposite Rajghat, in the Deyra Doon, with its waters as red as if they had been artificially mixed with red ochre, at a time, too, when the Jumna itself was as clear as crystal; the turbid water from the Girri keeping to the right, and running in a well-defined course for miles without mixing with the main stream.

crystal, and the boulder bed over which it passes is visible at great depths. The boulders and shingle gradually disappear at a point from twelve to sixteen miles below the debouch of the rivers from the Sewaliks, and from this they proceed onwards, through a trough or k'hadir, on a much reduced slope, over a bed of coarse quartzose sand, with a great admixture of mica, the latter ingredient being less abundant as the river advances.

It will be understood that the Ganges and Jumna, where the canals issue from them, are perennial in their supply, the Ganges up to that point having drained a vast tract of elevated mountain country by its two great branches (Bhageretti and Alukhnunda), both of which have their origin in the snow. The Jumna does the same on a less extended front. The fountain-head of the Ganges springs at the foot of that gorgeous mass of perpetual snow which forms so remarkable an object from the plains well known as Gungootri:[1] that of the Jumna from an equally well-known and conspicuous mass of snow, and perhaps more remarkable in its outline—Jumnootri.

Monsoon and Periodical Rains.—These water-supplies are greatly modified by local circumstances, and the effects of the south-west monsoon which, from the month of June to September, never fail. The influence of this south-west monsoon extends far into the interior of the Himalayas, through the gorges of the rivers, and over the crests of the massive mountain barrier which opposes it towards the plains. So continued is the rain at this period on these elevated ridges, that at Lundour and Mussoori I have known it to fall for weeks in succession, with only a slight cessation towards the evening, when the clouds from the interior which rolled over the ridge appeared to push back for a limited period the vapours

[1] The more distant is the Neelung beyond the snowy range.

which rose from the valleys and plains at the base. The vast supply that the great river must obtain at this period from the mountains may be estimated by the rain-gauge at Lundour, giving an annual return, on a mean of ten years, from 1850 to 1859, of 92·73 inches,[1] whilst those in the plains at Meerut and Delhi respectively give 20 and 30 inches only.

The irregular effects which are produced by local rainfalls on these rivers are not to be overlooked; and the sudden rises of floods quite independent of the supply from the interior of the mountains, and in fact equally independent of the monsoon, are elements of importance when the daily volume of water in the rivers becomes a matter of consideration.

Colonel Richard Strachey, Royal Engineers, in a paper on the Geology of the Himalaya, read before the London Geological Society, June 25, 1851, states—
" On one occasion I myself measured a fall of one inch
" of rain in about twenty minutes; this was at Hurdwar,
" where the Ganges leaves the outer hills."

Lieutenant Wilberforce Greathead, Royal Engineers, in a report on the drainage of the city of Delhi in 1852, at p. 3 gives an instance of a fall of rain in that city, 6th August, 1851, of 1 inch per hour for two consecutive hours. On September 29th and 30th, 1850, at Dhunowri (a canal post in the Ganges k'hadir, situated five miles south of the Sewaliks), rain fell from 8 P.M. to 6 A.M. 8·40 inches, and from 6 A.M. to 6 P.M., 4·81 inches, or 13·21 inches in twenty-four hours. At Dadoopoor, on the Western Jumna Canal, the heaviest fall of rain in fifteen years during twenty-four hours is shown to be 13·04 inches; but the quantity of rain that falls at Dadoopoor and Dhunowri is influenced by their proximity to moun-

[1] See *Report of the Sanitary State of the Army in India.*—Vol. ii., p. 134.

tain and forest ranges. Taking the average of six years from 1844–45 to 1849–50 inclusive, I find that the fall of rain at Delhi was thus:—

Maximum fall...... 28·77 inches in the year 1849-50.
Minimum fall...... 14·92 „ in the year 1848-49.
Mean in 6 years... 18·36 „

At Meerut—

Maximum fall...... 38·51 inches in the year 1849-50.
Minimum fall...... 23·43 „ in the year 1848-49.
Mean in 6 years... 30·66 „

I append a register kept at Dadoopoor from the year 1834 to 1848, which, through a period of fifteen years, gives much interesting information as regards the rainfall in that locality:—

REGISTER OF THE RAIN-GAUGE KEPT AT DADOOPOOR,
From 1st January, 1834 to 31st December, 1848.

Years.	Jan.	Feb.	Mar.	Apr.	May.	June.	July	Aug.	Sept.	Oct.	Nov.	Dec.	Total.
	Inch.	Inch.	Inch.	Inch.	Inch.	Inch.	Inch.	Inch.	Inch.	Inch.	Inch.	Inch.	Inches.
1834....	..	..	..	..	..	1·85	25·36	8·35	11·63	3·64	..	0·95	51·78
1835....	0·51	0·77	1·30	2·09	0·65	13·25	21·72	6·16	2·79	..	..	0·03	49·27
1836....	0·31	7·25	0·59	0·54	0·20	5·0	5·57	6·93	3·81	..	..	0·42	30·62
1837....	..	1·28	2·43	0·20	0·26	0·97	9·05	4·50	2·87	0·69	..	..	22·25
1838....	..	0·37	2·56	2·12	2·02	1·83	18·33	16·44	4·68	0·16	0·69	..	49·20
1839....	2·99	3·97	2·79	..	1·97	5·73	6·66	11·67	4·44	..	0·52	0·09	40·83
1840....	3·77	0·03	0·86	0·77	1·43	5·93	7·60	4·68	2·90	..	0·08	..	28·05
1841....	0·63	1·86	1·29	0·11	1·03	17·99	12·98	9·70	12·93	..	1·08	1·23	60·83
1842....	0·97	1·52	..	..	0·22	15·49	3·96	10·02	2·71	..	0·09	0·75	35·73
1843....	1·73	0·64	0·45	0·48	0·32	0·69	13·62	6·31	7·33	5·61	..	0·28	37·36
1844....	0·35	1·75	0·64	..	0·78	0·71	30·0	12·71	..	..	..	..	46·94
1845....	0·08	5·54	1·81	0·15	0·48	6·68	21·39	4·18	2·76	..	..	0·16	43·23
1846....	0·02	0·17	0·50	0·06	1·04	7·11	13·73	15·94	7·74	..	..	..	46·31
1847....	2·20	2·42	0·64	0·16	1·15	7·36	10·57	9·40	6·13	0·61	0·55	0·06	41·25
1848....	0·37	0·38	0·28	..	0·99	3·06	4·82	8·58	0·91	0·66	..	0·63	20·68
Total..	13·93	27·95	16·14	6·68	12·54	93·65	205·26	135·57	73·63	11·37	3·01	4·60	604·33
Average	0·928	1·863	1·076	0·445	0·836	6·243	13·684	9·038	4·908	0·758	0·200	0·306	40·288

Remarks on the above observations:—"I have noted that we have very heavy floods every seventh year thus:—In 1821, the ferry boat on the Jumna came over the Kadur lands to Kurnal station. In 1828, the Jumna bank work at Kulsera was destroyed. The Jumna and canal joined. In 1835, the Soomb weir entirely destroyed. The flood rose to 11′-3″ above dam floor. In 1842, the floods rose to 12′ above floor of dam, which nearly turned the dam. The greatest fall of rain in any 24 hours, during the above 15 years, has been 13·04 inches on 22nd June, 1842. On the 8th of June, 1841, the thermometer stood from 98° to 100° from 8 P.M. to 4 A.M. on the 9th. On the 4th of May, 1848, the thermometer having been exposed to the night air, stood at 67° at daylight, and at 1 P.M., in the same situation, it rose to 164° in the sun.

"W. DAWE,

"*Assistant Superintendent Western Jumna Canals.*

"*Camp Indree*, 11*th March*, 1849."

It would appear that in both 1821 and 1828 the Jumna River and the Canal under Kurnal were joined by the intervening k'hadir or low land being inundated. The width of this low land is between five and six miles. The extreme width of k'hadir from the right to left at this point is ten miles.

I would refer those who possess copies of the Ganges Canal report, to Plates 60 and 61 of the Atlas, in which there are tables of the curves of high and low water in the Ganges, at Futtigurh and Cawnpoor, for every day in the year, for eleven years. For those who have not got a copy of the Report I append the following abstracts :—

GANGES RIVER AT FUTTIGURH, *from* 1843 *to* 1853 *inclusive.*

Maximum height to which floods reached—

	Feet.	In.	
In 1843 above the level of 1 Jan. 1843 ...	9	4 ...	1 Aug.
1844 „ „ „	9	2 ...	19 „
1845 „ „ „	8	11 ...	31 July.
1846 „ „ „	10	8 ...	17 „
1847 „ „ „	8	9 ...	30 „
1848 „ „ „	9	3 ...	26 Aug.
1849 „ „ „	8	7 ...	20 „
1850 „ „ „	8	11 ...	24 „
1851 „ „ „	8	11 ...	12 July.
1852 „ „ „	9	4 ...	24 „
1853 „ „ „	9	10 ...	1 Aug.
	101	8	
Average height in 11 years........	9	2·9	

GANGES RIVER AT CAWNPOOR, *from* 1843 *to* 1853 *inclusive.*

Maximum height to which floods reached—

	Feet.	In.		
In 1843............	12	10	on	15 September.
1844............	12	11		6 ,,
1845............	12	5		1 August.
1846............	13	8		21 July.
1847............	12	0		14 August.
1848............	13	2		28 ,,
1849............	12	9		27 September.
1850............	12	5		4 October.
1851............	11	10		14 August.
1852............	12	7½		10 September.
1853............	12	7		27 July.
	139	2		
Average height in 11 years	12	7·81		

The action, therefore, on the head-works of the canals in these provinces must not be looked upon as limited to the volume of water which drains the Himalayas, but must be extended to the rain which falls at irregular periods in the neighbourhood—a consideration of infinite importance in estimating the danger to be apprehended from sudden overcharge; in fact, the suddenness with which floods come down the mountain torrents connected with the canal works in the northern Doab, or on that tract lying between the Ganges and Jumna rivers, is one of their most dangerous features. Men working upon the dam across the Muskurra River have been carried away before they could escape to the side platforms, and it has only been after long experience, and then not always with certainty, that the dam-sluices could be thrown open in time to receive the floods. The Muskurra at the point where the dam is situated, twelve miles from its debouch from the Sewaliks, runs on a slope of 9½ feet per mile; and the declivity of the sandy-bedded torrents in connection with the canal works, which they cross in some shape or other, on this line of country, may be estimated as varying on an average, taking lengths above and below the works, from 5 feet per mile to 25½ feet per mile; whilst the Ganges and Jumna, which run on beds of boulders and shingle, have a slope, at the points where the canal heads leave them, of 16 feet and between 20 and 30 feet per mile, respectively.

A long experience of these torrents and rivers led me to look to the 20th of June, or thereabouts, as the commencement of the flood season, and about this time the earlier floods invariably occur. Heavy floods followed in July, and frequently in August and September, after which the works were considered to be safe from any severe attack of this nature. The effect in augmented volume upon the great rivers, however, lasts until the end of October.

During the cold weather months, or from November until February, a lull takes place, broken at irregular or uncertain intervals by heavy falls of rain, which usually occur during the months of November, December, or January: these falls of rain (called the cold weather rains) lead to very severe floods, both in the Ganges and Jumna, although the rivers subside in the course of three or four days. The uncertainty of the period at which these floods may be expected to take place is a constant source of anxiety, and places unfinished works, situated in the bed of the rivers, in great jeopardy.

Melting of the Snow, and Effects thereof.—In March the melting of the snow in the Higher Himalayas again brings surplus water into the great rivers, which lasts, with little intermission, until the commencement of the monsoon; so that, in fact, from November until March, or say for five months (during which period heavy floods occur at irregular intervals), the rivers are free, or only partially free, from floods. These are facts to be considered when estimating the difficulties and cost of building permanent works in connection with them, and I may observe that they have been well considered by engineers whose local experience has been brought to bear upon the subject.

Sewalik Hills, and Beds of Rivers.—With reference to the Sewalik Hills, and the beds of the great rivers, as affording a supply of material for building purposes, I will before closing this part of my paper, which is descriptive of the Ganges and Jumna as connected with the mountain regions, explain that the Sewaliks, which separate the valley of Deyra from the plains, consist of an uninterrupted range of high broken ridges or hills, the extreme elevation of which above the sea does not exceed 3,140 feet.[1] Its length from the Ganges to the Jumna is forty-six miles, and its width about six miles, closed at the Jumna extremity by perpendicular cliffs bounding the bed of the river, but open to the valley of Deyra on the Ganges, at Hurdwar, by a carriage road. Intermediately there are various passes more or less accessible; the most familiar of which are the Timli, Kheeri or Lal Durwaza (the height of which above the level of the sea at the station of Shorepoor is 2,606·31 feet) and the Khas Rao Pass. The whole formation is tertiary of the miocene period. It consists of a series of boulder beds, sand, and clays in various states of induration, upheaved at an angle of 15° to 25°, and with the exception of that portion near Hurdwar, at which there is a remarkable fault, by which the dip is reversed, the inclination is towards the valley of Deyra, or to the north-east. The best idea that I can give of this series of stata is, that were the existing beds of the Ganges and Jumna to be upheaved, they would represent in their succession of

[1] Amsot Peak, Timli Pass, 3,139 ft. 8 in., say 3,140 ft.

boulders and sand, those which we now have in the Sewaliks. It is marvellous to see with what pertinacity these beds of rounded stones, many of them equal in bulk to 2 and 6 cubic feet, withstand at the highest and most critical points of these elevated mountains the weathering of the climate. Points and pinnacles, topped by the pine-tree (*Pinus longifolia*) indigenous to the soil, hold their own against the heaviest storms and the most protracted rains, the shingle and boulder beds of which they are composed, not being in a state of agglutination or in a hard matrix, but merely embedded in the sand in which they were upheaved.

In the sandstone, remains of the larger mammalia have been discovered, and in the clay bed underlying the boulder and sand strata, a very interesting series of remains of both mammalia and reptiles was collected by me in the Kalowala Pass, accompanied by lignite. Amongst these were horse, ruminants, rodents, crocodiles, tortoises, &c., &c.

There are in these mountains, no doubt, occasional nuclei or embedded masses of compact coarse-grained sandstone solidified by calcareous cement, and also of agglutinated conglomerate; but, as a general rule, the rock is worthless for common purposes. During my sojourn in the neighbourhood, and especially in my younger days, when I was detached to the passes, and remained there for months, wandering into every accessible ravine, valley, or river, that I could find, with my gun and geological hammer as companions, I had more opportunities than most men of observing and studying the character of the formation, and the quality of the materials that composed it. I have met with the sandstone, very rarely so hard that it would strike fire with steel, and of that peculiar character which those who are experienced in the larger fossils know to exist when in contact with them. In my pamphlet replying to Sir Arthur Cotton's strictures on the Ganges Canal Works, I have used the term "crystalline" as expressing the nature of this variety: the term was intended merely as an exponent of apparent compactness, and was not meant as "formed of crystals," or connected with crystallization in any shape. I have been warned of the probability that the use of this term may be misunderstood, I therefore take the earliest opportunity of correcting and explaining it.

In the slips that occur during the rainy months huge masses of the sandstone rock are precipitated into the bed of the torrents. During their descent, and on their coming in contact with the bed, the greater portion resolves itself into its original elements, and, with the exception of the more indurated parts, is washed away. The harder nuclei are those selected by the natives in building at Hurdwar and Kunkhul; they are stripped of their outer unconsolidated surface, and their harder interior is carried, at great expense, and with much trouble, to the stonebuilder. At Badshahmuhul, a very extensive palace, situated on a branch of the Jumna below the Kharra Head, built in Shah Juhan's time, a great deal of this stone has been used, and the effect that weathering has had upon it may be seen by any one who visits the place; but it is significant, that in all the ornamented and finished parts of the building the architect has rejected the Sewalik and used the sandstone of the Agra district. The river face of this old palace is on its whole basement, constructed of boulders laid in cement; and masses of the building now lie prostrate in the bed of the river, bearing the character of natural conglomerate rather than artificial building. At various other places in the neighbourhood of these mountains the sandstone has been used, but its use only shows how incapable it is of standing weathering, much less the attrition and solvent power of water containing carbonic acid, and the action of such water as would pass over the falls or dams on the canal works.

The boulders and shingle (generally consisting of masses of the older rocks, worn down and rounded by constant attrition, with a comparatively small proportion of limestone), which constitute the beds of these rivers, afford an infinite supply of material for the solid portions of works on which they can be delivered economically. They have been very largely used both in the headworks of the canals on the Ganges and Jumna Rivers, and have been carried to considerable distances down their courses, not only for building purposes, but also for the protection of the foundations and platforms of bridges and falls. On the Ganges Canal especially, the whole of the boulders taken from the excavation from Myapoor downwards, as well as those gathered from the beds of the rivers in the vicinity, have been used in the foundation of the headworks, bridges, superpassages, and falls in the k'hadir, to an extent only limited by the means of carriage; and as my project (as explained in the *Ganges Canal Report*) contemplated a protective flooring of two feet in depth to the whole of the earthen aqueduct across the Solani Valley, besides stones of this description at the various falls and bridges, not only above, but below, Roorkee, all of which are protected with this most invaluable material, there can be no doubt of the consideration that I have given to it.

The Zumeendars at Raipoor, on the Jumna, as well as those at Kunkhul, on the Ganges, used in former days to draw a considerable revenue from leasing tracts of the shingle beds of the rivers to lime-burners. A very profitable trade was carried on by this class of people in collecting the limestone boulders, and, as fuel was plentiful, in burning them on the spot, and either selling the lime to the public works, or carrying it on Bunjarra[1] bullocks to great distances south, even as far as Meerut, where a sale could be found for it.

Both on the Ganges and Jumna Canals, lime, obtained from this source, has been the best that we have been able to procure. The limestone boulders vary in quality, many of them being of the purest crystalline texture, whilst others are more or less argillaceous; this combination of the pure with clay varieties produced an hydraulic cement of the greatest value.[2]

In short, both the limestone boulders, as well as those of other denominations, have been used for so long a period, so largely, and have been so highly prized as useful and valuable material on the canal works in the North-Western Provinces, that I look with surprise and astonishment on (at this the eleventh hour) being called to account for remissness in not only not having used them on the works, but having overlooked their value: a reproach which is not only deliberately made by Sir Arthur Cotton, in his report to the East India Irrigation Company, but persisted in in his rejoinder to my pamphlet, after I had told him that he was mistaken.

Before dismissing this part of the subject, there are two points so characteristic of the manner in which Sir Arthur Cotton deals with matters before him, as to demand

---

1 Bunjara—*Elliot.*

2 On the lower tracts of the Eastern Jumna Canal I used the "stone lime," as it is called—viz., lime obtained from the boulders in the upper regions of the Jumna, at the canal head, with an admixture of "bujree," or coarse red sharp angular sand, highly impregnated with iron-oxyd, which is found in large quantities at Delhi. This, in the proportion one part of lime to one and even two parts of bujree, was, at that time, considered one of the best cements procurable on the canals.

special notice. In his so-called Private Memorandum, p. 48 "Reply to Statements," he refers to the abundance of boulders (by him called pebbles) in the river bed of the Ganges, adapted for rubble masonry, in terms which, taken along with the context, imply that they had not been so employed by me, and that it was left to him to indicate their use. In my reply (p. 14 as above), I briefly stated that "a great portion of the solid work of most "of the canal buildings in the k'hadir has been con-"structed with this material." Regardless of this correction, General Cotton, in his rejoinder, after referring to my illustration of the ancient rubble masonry of the basement of the Badshah Mahul palace, reiterates his charge in the following terms:—"It seems very strange that "with such a hint they (the boulders) were not generally "used when there were unlimited supplies on the spot," p. 59, and he argues upon this assumption. The material in question was *most* extensively used and, wherever it could be had, applied in the headworks, in the foundations of bridges, falls, and platforms, where, being covered by either earth, masonry or water, it is not always visible. Nowise moved, Sir Arthur Cotton persists in his disproved statements. "He (Sir Proby Cautley) also says those peb-"bles were used in some of the works, but it must have "been a very small proportion, for *I saw no pebble masonry*, "nor was it ever mentioned or alluded to in the long "discussions I had with the officers on the spot," p. 94. He might, upon the same grounds, deny that hoop iron was used in the masonry of the blocks which support the Solani aqueduct, or that the standard imperial pound and the current coins of the realm had been imbedded in the foundation stone of the Palace of Westminster.

The next matter is of a still graver complexion. It refers to Sir Arthur Cotton's authoritatively given professional opinion regarding the Sewalik sandstone. In his strictures on the use of brick, he says:—"I had "always *supposed* that the only great objection to it "was *the want of stone,* and I was astonished beyond "measure, to find the most unexceptional stone in the "streets of Hurdwar, which, I was informed, had been "brought only six miles, and many of the houses built "of stone. What could have been the reason for "rejecting this invaluable material, the very thing that "was wanted for the works, I am still totally at a loss "to conceive," p. 47 "Reply to Statements." Upon these premises he continues the argument of his strictures: —"I saw some of just the requisite degree of hardness; "quite sufficiently hard to resist water, and, at the same "time, not needlessly hard, so as to involve an unneces-"sary expense in cutting," p. 48 as above. "If *quarries* "*are now opened in the sub-Himalayas, there would, doubt-*"*less, be, in a short time, a prodigious traffic in stone, along* "*the whole line of the canal,*" p. 48 as above. The italics here, as elsewhere, are General Cotton's. In my reply, I stated, after some details, that, "as a rule, however, "the Sewalik sandstone is notoriously inferior, as a "material for building, but that some of the best quality "had been used in the Myapoor Regulating-bridge," p. 13 as above. In his rejoinder, Sir A. Cotton says:— "Sir Proby Cautley next answers my objection *to the* "*sole use of bricks when excellent stone was to be had close* "*to Hurdwar.* He first says that he does not object "so much to brick masonry as I do, yet adds, no "man in his senses would select brick when good stone "was to be had at a reasonable price." p. 92. Sir Arthur Cotton then goes on to state how he had used sandstone at the Godaveri works, where the material was of every degree of hardness, and where he had, consequently, to select the hard stone for particular parts. He reiterates his opinion of the Sewalik sandstone in the following terms:—"That there was most excellent stone, "perfectly fitted for the works, on the spot, is certain, "for I saw large blocks of it lying in the street of "Hurdwar, intended for some building, and which, I "was informed, *had been brought* only six miles. I have "pieces of this stone with me now," p. 93. Again, "These facts were simple and undeniable, viz., that the "officers were entirely at a loss for the failure of the "brickwork, while there was, on the spot, excellent "stone, which I saw and examined in company with "the officers of the works. *My professional opinion was, "and is, that had this stone been used in those works, there "would not have been the smallest anxiety about them,"* p. 95. The italics are Sir Arthur Cotton's. It shall now be my duty to show how this solemnly stated professional opinion may be open to question, bearing in mind that the material is to be used in heavy hydraulic works, for floorings or pavements exposed to large masses of water running over them with great velocity, and that he successively designates it as—"Good stone (Calcutta "lecture); Most unexceptional stone; Invaluable mate"rial; Of just the requisite degree of hardness; Most "excellent stone;" and that, when at Hurdwar, he never saw the so-called quarries, only six miles off, out of which it came.

A great part of the continent of India is covered by a formation of sandstone, the most extensively distributed of all the secondary deposits occurring there, and developed in great force. It extends as far south as the Nagerry hills, in the Eastern Ghats, W.N.W. of Madras; to Cutch on the west and to the Rajmahal hills on the east. It is seen flanking the northern and western sides of the Trap district of Malwa; on the Bundair hills of Bundelkund, and stretching to the utmost limits of the Vindhya range. It occurs along the western banks of the Jumna, from Delhi to Allahabad, and thence to Monghir. In Bundelkund it forms a great plateau, described by Dangerfield, Jacquemont, and others. It occurs near the Godaveri and on the banks of the Kistna, where it attains an enormous thickness. This great formation, *the Punna or Bundela Sandstone*, presents itself very frequently as a metamorphic rock; commonly it is a fine-grained, compact, red, grey or white sandstone, of extreme hardness and durability, either for hydraulic works or for building purposes. Where it occurs in any considerable thickness, it is often variable in quality; the superior strata being hard and compact, while the lower are occasionally more or less friable; but the harder description is always to be met with. For building purposes it is usually equal to the best kinds of the "old red sandstone" of the British Isles. In the neighbourhood of Delhi this sandstone is fine-grained, excessively compact and silicious. It has been employed there in the construction of ancient monuments of the most enduring character. The geological age of this vast formation of Indian sandstone has been inferred to be Oolitic, at the very latest, if not of a more ancient secondary period. Such is the rock occurring in the valley of the Godaveri, and on the banks of the Kistna, which General Cotton, with long experience of its use, had as a standard of comparison when his attention was directed to what he calls "the most excellent stone" of the Sewalik hills.

Let us now see what that stone really is. The Sewalik hills, in consequence of being so rich in mammalian fossil remains, have been examined throughout, between the Ganges and the Jumna, and between the Jumna and the Sutlej, with an amount of painstaking observation such as has probably never been applied to any other range of hills in India, or to any range out of Europe. They have been successively explored and described by myself, Dr. Falconer, Victor Jacquemont, Colonel Strachey, and Mr. Medlicott. Instead of being geologically of "middle secondary" age, they are of the newer tertiary, or what is called "upper miocene." Regarded in their *ensemble*, they consist of unconsolidated beds of sand, clays, and boulder-gravel, or of loosely consolidated and crumbling sandstones, which imbibe water to saturation, and weather with disintegration very rapidly, together with beds of conglomerate more or less loosely aggregated. The lowermost strata of the section near the mouths of the Timli and Kalowala Passes have yielded teeth, molars and incisors of the horse, rodents, and other mammalia—all of the miocene age. Falconer, Jacquemont, and Strachey have all agreed in describing the strata as being of this incoherent character.[1] Occasionally, as I have above stated, imbedded masses of a more compact texture occur, which effervesce freely with acids, arising from a calcareous paste; or they may be consolidated with an argillaceous base, so as to produce a material like that which I refer to as having been used at the Myapoor Regulating-bridge, and if I recollect rightly, in the cutwaters of the Solani aqueduct; but such blocks are procured with difficulty at points detached and far distant, and at an expense which, when my works were in progress, I did not consider myself justified in incurring, more especially as I had no faith in the value of the stone, nor in its durability. No doubt that, as compact masses have been found with great trouble and at great expense,

---

[1] *Vide* Appendix. Jacquemont does not admit that the indurated sands are sufficiently consolidated to deserve the name of *sandstone:* but this is an extreme opinion.

further trouble and expense will produce stone of the same quality; but I warn the engineers against introducing the Sewalik sandstone upon the works, without the greatest care and the most vigilant scrutiny. At Hurdwar, Kunkhul, and Juwallapoor, the material is used by the natives for building purposes, from the convenience of its immediate vicinity, as slab and block kunkur of modern origin have been largely used in the Ganges Canal works in the Bolundshuhur and Mynpoori districts, as well as elsewhere, by the natives under similar circumstances. But although the passes and ravines of the Sewalik hills are ransacked for gums, dyes, bamboos, and timber; and although excellent lime is procured and exported, by burning the limestone boulders occurring in the beds of the rivers of the Deyra Doon, not a square foot of sandstone is ever exported from the Sewalik hills into the towns of the adjoining plains for building purposes. I do not believe that a single house is to be met with from the Sutlej at Roopur to the Ganges, with the exception of those at Hurdwar, Kunkhul, and places in the immediate vicinity of these hills, built of the Sewalik sandstone. Be it remembered that the Delhi crystalline sandstone, and that of the Agra district, are extensively used, and sent to long distances by the natives, who have a sharp and practised eye to building materials.

Fragments taken from indurated masses, left after an "*éboulement*" of soft chalk from the cliffs of Dover, would not justify the assertion that quarries of "most "valuable stone" existed there, capable of supplying a "prodigious traffic," and suited for the uses to which mountain limestone is supplied. Yet this is what General Cotton has done in comparing the comparatively modern soft sandstone of the Sewalik hills with the old sandstone rock of the south of India, which, as a rule, is exceedingly hard and singularly durable.[1]

Northern Doab and Rivers after leaving the Highlands.—The description above given applies to the Ganges and Jumna Rivers down to their debouch into the plains through the Sewaliks; it embraces, therefore, all the mountainous regions, with the Sewaliks and the beds of rivers, as connected with the supply of building materials for the works. The remaining portion of the paper will be devoted to the plains and flat country, or to that strip which (under the name of the Northern Doab) is bounded on the East by the Ganges and on the West by the Jumna, terminating at Allahabad, where the two rivers effect a junction. I shall enter more especially upon the nature of the rivers, the extensive k'hadirs or troughs through which they run, and on the levels of the high land with their relative bearings to those of the rivers themselves. In the first place, however, I must remove any impression from the mind of the reader that the high land which I am about to describe is a Delta[2] in the true geographical signification of that term.

Deltas.—The word "Delta" is carelessly used as descriptive of a tract of country bounded by two rivers above their junction; and in this signification the term "Delta of the Ganges and Jumna" has been frequently made use of as expressive of the land lying between these two rivers.

When, however, we enter into a critical disquisition

---

[1] *See* Appendix A., giving copy *in extenso* of my reply to General Cotton on the use of brick. "Reply to Statements," p. 12 to 15, and authorities quoted on the sandstone of the Sewalik Hills.

[2] See p. 53 of my pamphlet, "Reply to Statements," 1863. "Supposing the land in the centre of the Delta is 50 feet above," &c., writes Sir Arthur Cotton, in his so-called Private Memorandum to the East India Irrigation Company.

on the rivers connected with the Ganges and Jumna Canals, and draw a comparison between their capabilities and those of the Godaveri and Kistna, we must be more precise in our language. As bearing upon the latter, and with reference to its true meaning, the term "Delta" as applied to the land in which the canals of the north-west run, is quite inappropriate. The true Deltaic segment of a river (like the Godaveri, Kistna, &c.) has not only a slope on its right and left banks parallel to its course, but also a transverse slope *outwards* from the central ridge on which the river itself runs; so that the Deltaic channels actually run *above* the surface of the country, and as it were between embankments formed in the process of ages by the deposition of silt. It is this peculiar attribute of the Deltaic segments of rivers which has won for them the character of being the best adapted and most easily worked upon for irrigation purposes.[1]

The Ganges and the Jumna, on the contrary, run in deep troughs below the surface, the country on each side having a slope parallel to their courses, but with a transverse slope *inwards,* so that each river has its own watershed, pouring from a ridge intermediately situated. It will be understood, therefore, that in these high regions the true Deltaic channel does not exist; to look for that of the Ganges we must descend to the latitude of Rajmahal, 400 miles below the tract of country now under review. "About 220 miles from the sea (but 300, reckon-" ing the windings of the river,) commences the head of " the *Delta* of the Ganges," says Rennell in his account of this great river.[2]

1 *See* the map of the Delta of the Godaveri, Plate II., which accompanies this paper, reproduced from Colonel Baird Smith's report.

2 *See* p. 258. Memoir of a Map of Hindustan, by J. Rennell, F.R.S. *Major of Engineers,* &c.

IDEAL SECTION ACROSS A DELTA.

Springs.—There is a remarkable phenomenon with reference to springs at the foot of the Sewaliks which deserves mention before we proceed to a description of the plain country. In the immediate vicinity of the passes, and at the foot of the hills, spring water rises to the surface, sometimes exhibiting itself in mere pools, at other times in small streams and rills, which flow for a short distance and then disappear in the sand and shingle of the bed of the river. Parallel to and south of this line, is a belt varying from five to ten miles in breadth, in which water can only be reached at extreme and, in some cases, unmanageable depths.

In advance of this dry belt, the springs rise to or near the surface, forming in Rohilkund the unhealthy tract called the Turai. In the Doab, a decrease in the depth of wells marks the approach to the belt in question; although on a line traceable from Badshahpoor near Dhunowri to the southern angle of that part of the Ganges k'hadir with which the canal works are connected, the existence of detached, and in some cases extensive, jheels and marshes assimilates the surface to that of the Rohilkund Turai. The cause of this peculiarity is, that in the whole of the tract skirting the mountains, there is a deep-seated impervious stratum rising near the foot of the hills, and cropping out on the northern limit of the Turai belt; that the water passing down the rivers penetrates through the shingle, and, passing under this impervious stratum, rises again to the surface at a considerable distance, leaving the intermediate space dry.[1]

[1] Another, and, perhaps, a better explanation is given by Dr. Falconer, who supposes that the water percolates through the shingle, and

The above, which is an extract from my report on the Ganges Canal works, is illustrated by the following. The Jumna at its debouch from the Sewaliks has a discharge per second equal to 4,000 cubic feet. During the dry months it occasionally happens that the whole of this water disappears at a point below the canal heads; it is partly taken off by lateral cuts into the Delhi Canal on the West, and into the Eastern Jumna Canal on the East, strong bunds being thrown across the bed of the river to effect this object; the portion which is not admitted into the canal cuts, escapes unobservedly through the shingle. South, or on the down-stream side of these bunds, the bed of the Jumna has been laid perfectly dry, and to a distance of some miles south no appearance of springs of any description has existed. Long before the river has reached the parallel of Suharunpoor, however, water again appears, and although fordable at certain points, boats are required at all the ghats and ferries for the transport of merchandise. Opposite Agra the river is so far navigable, that boats varying from 500 to 1000 maunds (18 to 36 tons,) laden with cotton, leave that place for the lower provinces, and as far as I could discover from inquiry amongst the boat people, the difficulty that they experienced was not in the neighbourhood of Agra, but immediately above the junction of the Chumbul, where the Jumna forms a shallow rapid, and during the dry months offers an impediment, although not an insurmountable one to the passage of craft.

The average transverse section of the Jumna at Agra during the driest months may be estimated at 900 superficial feet, that is to say the breadth is 300 and the hydraulic mean depth is 3 feet. The slope of

is stopped, at great depths, by an impervious clay stratum, along which *it runs, until* the stratum of clay crops out on the surface.

the river is about 1·25 feet per mile; the discharge, therefore, is 2,061 cubic feet per second.

General description of Troughs or K'hadirs.—The rivers within the northern Doab, as well as the Ganges and Jumna, by which that Doab is bounded, run in *k'hadirs* or troughs (*vide* cut), of widths varying from 1 to 10 or even 13 miles.

IDEAL SECTION ACROSS K'HADIR SIX MILES WIDE.

This *k'hadir* or low country has been gradually scooped out at early periods through the higher lands, below which it is situated at considerable depths, varying on the line to which my description is limited from about 45 to 100 feet or upwards. The boundaries are marked either by high banks or scarps on one side, with shelving slopes on the other, or by well-defined scarps on both sides.

This low land or k'hadir is the wide channel within which the river is restlessly employed in changing its position—one year here, another year there, but its movements are strictly confined within the limits that have been assigned to it. In the boulder and shingle-region to the north, the rivers are divided into widely detached streams by islands covered with Sissoo (*Dalbergia sissoo*) and are not unfrequently in parts well cultivated, whilst the lowland on the flanks is marked by morass and reed jungle, the resort of elephants, tigers, and other wild animals. These morasses extend to the region considerably south, but through the whole tract, both north and south, the surface is reticulated by nullas and swamps. Large tracts of this k'hadir are under cultivation, and it is in part studded with villages holding the richest and best lands in the districts. These villages are if possible placed on an elevated patch; but although the general level of the surface is above the high-water mark of the usual rains, a slight rise caused by severe floods which periodically happen, does much damage, and inundates enormous tracts of k'hadir land. The rich soil, so valuable in agriculture, is entirely superficial; it is underlaid by sand to immense depths: the whole extent and breadth of the k'hadir being in fact a basin of sand, with here and there beds of a more fruitful soil deposited on the surface. There is much *duldul* quagmire or quicksand, especially in the northern regions, and connected with the morasses and reed-jungle, with a good deal of sand drift, especially during the March winds and the period of the north-westers; in short, the beds of the rivers have obtained a character of being the most treacherous, whilst the course of the rivers, in their advance through the k'hadir, is in the highest degree capricious.

Without speculating to any great extent on the *action* of rivers running under various circumstances, there can be no doubt that water in a large body passing *from* the high lands and mountain ranges upon Deltas, and borne superficially above the surface of the country (embanking itself, as it were, in its progress to the ocean), is under conditions very different from those which apply to torrents proceeding *through* the high lands, with their deeply-carved channels and their precipitous descents.

In the one case debacles and exaggerated floods, which occur periodically, are met by the relief caused by banks being overtopped, weak points giving way, and in either event leading to extensive lateral inundations which are well known in all low countries, but which relieve the main channel, and pass off on the subsidence of flood. In the other case, the masses of water being confined within the limits of a contracted channel, and not having the means of lateral escape, act upon the sides and bed of that channel with an intensity that is not exerted otherwise.

Here I consider we have the distinction between the action on Deltas like those of the Godaveri, &c., in Madras, and that on the rivers of the North-west running in Troughs. In the above few words I read the difference of action that would take place on a dam or raised obstruction built on the Godaveri, in its *Deltaic region*, and one built on the Ganges, in its *Trough region*,—relief in the first case being provided, under violent floods, by lateral inundations; in the second case, action being limited to a comparatively narrow channel, beyond which the water cannot escape—the torrent within those limits operates with unrestrained violence.

Should this be true as regards the distinctive character of rivers in their Deltaic and Trough regions, these regions will require very different treatment by the engineer. Works of the same description and detail will not answer for both. There may be a question as to such being at all applicable to both cases, but at any rate, when calculating estimates of cost, it would be dangerous to place them in the same category as to extent and proportions.

The above being a general description of the k'hadir of the rivers, I will now give a rapid sketch, in mere outline, of those of the Ganges and Jumna, terminating them at Allahabad, beyond which this paper is not interested.

Trough or K'hadir of the Ganges River.—Commencing with the Ganges at the point where the Ganges Canal head is placed, above the town of Hurdwar, the river is from one to one-and-a-half miles in width. Down to the village of Nagul, in the neighbourhood of which the shingle beds cease, there is, after the gorge of the hills is passed, a high bank on the right as far as Bhogpoor, below which the k'hadir opens out on both sides, to a great width, embracing the Asoffgurh Jheel, which lies to the East, where it is bounded by a steep and precipitous bank, and on the West by the low lands of the Solani valley, which are of extraordinary extent, and with drainage which will be fully explained when I enter on the description of the canals as connected with the water-shed and drainage of the high lands of the Northern Doab itself. On passing the mouths of the Solani, the width of the k'hadir is contracted to 1½ or 2 miles, the river itself running on very wide beds of sand, under the high bank on which stands the Sookurtal Fort. In advance of this, the k'hadir is greatly increased in width as shown by a line of old Ganges running on the right, and under the continuation of the high banks and sand-hills upon and amongst which Sookurtal stands. This old branch continues at a distance from the present river of about 5 miles, until it reaches the Ghurmuktesur Ghat and town, situated 95 miles below Hurdwar. The high bank and sand hills continue onwards passing the town of Pooth, at the west of which they curve inwards towards the river, which runs or used to run directly under the town. Independently of this expanse of k'hadir of 5 miles, on the right bank, that on the left, on the Bijnour and Moradabad side, is very extensive. I am informed by a friend who was for many years collector of revenue of Bijnour and also of Budaon, and who naturally took great interest in the action of the river in the low lands, that the maximum and minimum width of the k'hadir throughout these districts, extending in the first case from the debouch of the Ganges to a point 80 miles south, and in the second from opposite Ahar in the Bolundshuhur district to Kumpil, in the district of Futtigurh, on a line of 90 miles, could not be estimated at less than 10 and 5 miles. The towns of Pooth, Fureeduh, Ahar, Anoopshuhur, Kurumbas, Rajghat, are close upon the right bank of the k'hadir, which in the neighbourhood of these places extends back into the Budaon district. Below Rajghat, another old line of the Ganges marks the right limit of the k'hadir; this runs by Puttiali, Kumpil, and Shumshabad, to Futtigurh, at which point the present stream of the Ganges is close under the town and cantonment. The width of k'hadir between the old and existing Ganges is at one point near Puttiali and Khadirgunj, on the main river, not less than 12 or 13 miles, exclusive of the lowlands in the Budaon district on the East. Not far from this point, at a distance of about 2 miles, the Yar Wooffadar takes its course, forming a junction with the Ganges, lower down to the north-east, and opposite Shumshabad. On all this line, as far south as Futtigurh, the nature of the k'hadir is very uncertain, at parts very wide, studded with numerous villages, but broken up by low jheel and morass, with a reticulation of nullahs. Below Futtigurh, and on to Cawnpoor, the sandy bed of the river increases in extent, the k'hadir varying in width, and showing itself in vigorous proportions at those points in connection with the East Kalli Nuddi, Eesun, and Noon Rivers, which join the Ganges on the right bank above Cawnpoor. Nearly opposite the junction of the East Kalli Nuddi, about 50 miles above Cawnpoor, the Ramgunga enters the main stream of the Ganges. Owing to the influx of various rivers, the bed of the main Ganges, from Cawnpoor to Allahabad, is much increased in extent, and the sandy tracts bear a larger proportion to the superficial area of the k'hadir than they have done before. The town of Cawnpoor stands on the right bank of the Ganges, close under which the river runs, the low land on the left (or Oude side) being very extensive. As far as my recollection goes, the high bank maintains its position on the right, along the greater part of the distance to Allahabad; the left boundary of the k'hadir, and consequent inundation on the rise of the river being much more extensive on the Oude or left side. There are, however, exceptions, as at Singhour, Dalamow, Manikpoor, and other points where the main Ganges takes to the left, and where the banks are high.

We now turn to the Jumna River, with its k'hadir.

Trough or K'hadir of the Jumna.—The Jumna, as I have before said, leaves the Sewaliks in lat. 30° 21′ N., and 27 miles further north than the point where the Ganges enters on the plain country. After passing Kulesur and the Kharra Head, the k'hadir expands to a great width, the river dividing itself into numerous channels, connected more or less with the heads of supply for the canals. One of these, denominated the Boodhi Jumna, branches off on the East below Fyzabad, and fed by the Kharra Head channels, delivers the Eastern Jumna Canal supply on the Boodhi Jumna dam. Another, the Western branch, is the channel of main supply for the Western Jumna Canal on its leaving the main stream. The boulders and shingle cease at a point on the main stream above the latitude of Dadoopoor, and the course of the river continues on a bed of sand. Looking to the extent of the k'hadir on this line, we have on the East, extending from Nyashuhur, or say from the Kharra Head, a well-defined high bank, or (to use the native term for the boundaries of the k'hadir) *Danda*, marked by numerous large towns—Chilkhana, Sirsawa, Luknowti, Nukoor, &c., situated on its crest, extending as far south as Kurnal, which is situated 60 miles below Kulesur: at this point and opposite Kurnal the width of the k'hadir is 10 miles, nor is it at any point above Kurnal less than this. This low tract, the greater portion of which lies on the East of the river, is marked by wide and deep nullas, as well as by extensive marshes and jheels, although it is extensively cultivated in parts, and studded with villages. Putehur, which gives its name to a purgunah, is situated in this low land. The Nukoor and other jheels in the Suharunpoor district, well known as first-rate snipe ground, are in this part of the k'hadir. Here we have the main river constantly varying its course, separating portions of land and villages from the district to which they belong, and causing much injury to individual interests. The progress of a change of this sort came under my observation in the k'hadir lying between the Choki Station at Kulsea, on the Eastern Jumna Canal, and Dadoopoor, the head-quarter station in those days of the Western Jumna Canal; a straight cut across country, where the Jumna was fordable in the dry months. I had observed in two successive years that a low disconnected set of shallow jheels which had evidently at some previous time been connected with the main river, but which had always, in my frequent visits, been perfectly dry, had assumed a soft and spongy character, the second year exhibiting the change to a more marked extent than the previous one. On the third year I found myself most unexpectedly stopped on the edge of a channel running like a mill-stream, and in its course forcing away the sides bit by bit in the most formidable manner. The Jumna had, in fact, taken to a line in full force, which for the last two years had been adapting itself for its reception. The channel was so narrow that I held a conversation with people on the opposite side with the greatest ease. Its width did not at that time exceed 120 feet, but for the time it entirely prevented my progress to Dadoopoor.

Not far from this, in the lowlands of the Sooltanpoor Purgunah, a marsh had been gradually and imperceptibly forming in the vicinity of the drainage received in the k'hadir from the Nogong and Muskurra, two mountain torrents that cross the Eastern Jumna Canal Works. This marsh (with deposits of silt with which it was connected) became so formidable, and was extending itself over so much valuable land, that the revenue officers called upon the canal authorities to report upon its origin, and to make some arrangements either to prevent its further extension, or, if this were not possible, to drain it. Capt. Morton, of the Engineers, who was then chief of the Eastern Jumna Canal, took up the question with his usual ability, and by a system of well laid out drainage, most completely eradicated the evil. The cause, however, was this. The dams over the two mountain torrents to which I have above alluded, both of which were on very high slopes, had from their earlier existence in 1830 suffered from heavy retrogression of levels upon their tail platforms. In other words, the beds of the torrents, below the sites of the dams, had been gradually scooped out by the erosion of the current, and lowered to a depth of as much as 18 feet at the tail platforms. To prevent further retrogression, retaining-dams had been built across the beds of the torrents, at points lower down in the channel. What had become of the enormous quantity of sand that had been swept out of the bed? It was supposed that this had been carried away in the rains by the Jumna, and that, at any rate, it would have found its way to the sandy bed of the main river. On the contrary, this huge mass of alluvial matter had been gradually depositing itself over a vast tract of lowland in the k'hadir, and during the course of twelve years had imperceptibly arrived at the condition in which it was first brought to the notice of the collector of the district.

From Kurnal to Delhi the river, in its present course, is tortuous, with a tolerably regular k'hadir, the eastern *Danda* of which lies at a distance of about 6 miles from the main river, as far south as Kyranuh and Panniput, about 20 miles below Kurnal. The k'hadir at this point, viz., opposite Kyranuh and Panniput, is not less, I imagine, than 10 miles in width. In advance, the Eastern *Danda* is generally close upon the main river, and never exceeds two miles when separated from it. On this are situated the towns of Kotanuh and Baghput; the main extent of k'hadir is here on the right bank. From Baghput, which is about 20 miles from Delhi, the high bank or *Danda* on the East gradually retreats inland, and at Looni, which is a town or village built on a lofty isolated mound in the k'hadir, the width is about 7 miles. At the village of Sikrani, where the lockage on the Eastern Jumna Canal commences, the k'hadirs of the Hindun and Jumna unite in an immense expanse of lowland, in which the town of Shahderuh and numerous villages are situated; Ghazioddeennuggur stands on the edge of the high land or *Danda* which bounds the Hindun river on its East. At Delhi, and on the right of the Jumna, at some distance on its approach to that city, the highland is close upon the right. In fact, the low ridge of rock which runs from the Goorgaon district and from the Kootub inpinges upon the river at Delhi: this ridge is pierced by the Western Jumna Canal channel in its entrance to the city, and the Jumma Musjid is built upon it. An outlying mass of rock, upon which a fukeer's station used to be established,[1] was, in my time, on the left of the Jumna opposite Selimgurh, surrounded by the sandy bed of the river. The main stream passes not far from the Palace and Selimgurh (between which a branch runs), through a wide expanse of sand, with islands celebrated for the production of water-melons.

From Delhi to Agra, a distance of about 130 miles in a straight line, but very much more if the river is measured in all its tortuosities, the *Danda* or limit of the k'hadir continues on the left or East bank at some distance, with the exception of about five miles north of Jewur, where the high land approaches the river, its maximum not exceeding six miles, whilst on the right it is nearer the course of the river. At Nooh, on the left or East side, there is an extensive jheel, formed apparently by an old course of the Jumna, which in former years must have run in an extended curve inland. During the rains, and when the Jumna is at its height, this tract is inundated. Above Bindrabund there is k'hadir to, comparatively, a small extent on both banks of the river, but the town of Bindrabund itself is situated on the high bank upon the river, on a curve which passes round to Muttra. Muttra is also on the right edge of the river, with a considerable expanse of sand in front of it. Onwards to Agra, the Jumna assumes a very tortuous course, flanked by ravines which are perhaps more conspicuously shown on the right, until within about 20 miles of Agra, where these ravines are continuous on both sides, running up the course of the Kurroon river, which enters the Jumna on the left at

[1] This afforded large supplies of material for the works on the Eastern Jumna Canal, and was highly prized, as consisting of the glassy quartz rock of the Delhi formation.

the town of Shahderuh, about 20 miles below the Fort of Agra. From this point I should say, as far as my information extends, that the wide k'hadir to which we have been accustomed in the early part of the river's course gives place to a comparatively contracted bed, bounded by ravines of a most formidable character. The river, too, runs on a very tortuous course, and having received the Outunghun river on the right, arrives, after passing the fort and town of Etawah, at the junction of the Chumbul, a river which, rising in Malwa, near Mhow, has, on its reaching the Jumna, traversed a distance of 570 miles.

At the point of junction of these two great rivers the extent and intricacy of the ravines is most extraordinary. For a distance of at least twenty-five miles before their waters meet the whole of the intermediate tract (the rivers running nearly parallel), is one mass of entangled ravines; the width of the tract is at least five miles, which, in addition to the ravines on the right bank of the Chumbul and to those of the Koharri, another river running parallel, gives a wilderness of ravines extending in breadth to at least twelve miles. I am well acquainted with the river at Etawah, where the picturesque fort, a building of great antiquity, rises on the bank of the river, and where the tops of the ravines, as viewed from below, give a hilly outline, that reminded me of the Sewaliks. To compare these ravines with the Sewaliks is by no means exaggerating them, as far as their intricacy is concerned.

When standing on a high peak of the Sewaliks and looking down upon their length and breadth, you have before you a flat plateau apparently of elevated land, intersected by ravines and drainage, and reticulated to such an extent with a labyrinth of cliffs and watercourses, that it would be hopeless to endeavour to disentangle them. So it is with these wildernesses of ravines that occur on the Jumna,—they all represent the flat plateau on a level with the usual surface of the country, and they are all equally entangled in their topographical details. The Sewaliks, it is true, are elevated, whilst the Jumna ravines are on a level with the country in its neighbourhood; but the aspect of the latter from the bed of the river, which is situated 100 feet below, gives them a hilly outline, which is unmistakeable. At about 28 miles below Etawah (in a direct line, but nearly double that distance following the course of the river,) the united stream of the Sinde and Puhooj rivers joins the Jumna on the right, with a further complication of ravines, which are modified on the approach to, and at, Kulpee. Between the junction of the Chumbul at Kureem Khan, near Oorya, and some way above Kulpee, the channel at certain points is much interrupted by beds of kunkur, which have offered such serious obstructions to navigation that engineer officers have been employed in the clearance of channels, and, by removing the impediments, in greatly improving the navigation. In effecting this, which was done under the superintendence of Capt. Edward Smith, of the corps of Engineers, and Sergeant Deane, of the Sappers, some very interesting remains of the larger mammalia were discovered, a description of which, with a full account of the engineer's operation in the bed of the river, will be found in Vol. ii. page 622 of the *Journal of the Asiatic Society of Bengal*. Between this point and the town of Humeerpoor, 4 miles below which the Betwa River, on the right, forms a junction with the Jumna, the Etawah terminal of the Ganges Canal, and immediately above it the Seyngoor join the river on the right. At the point where the canal enters the Jumna the left bank is undulating, and on the 3rd January 1854, had a fall to the surface of the water of 98·08 feet, the high bank being on the opposite side with an intermediate stretch of sandy bed and low land of about 1½ miles between them. The character of the Seyngoor River on its junction with the Jumna, is similar to that of all the rivers in their connection with the main stream in this part of its course, tortuous and raviny, the ravines extending to a great width on the sides, and continuing far up the course of the tributary.

At a point 30 miles below the junction of the Betwa, the Kane river enters the Jumna on the right, and on the left between the Betwa and Kane, not far from the town of Jar, the Urrund or Rinde joins it on the left, with the usual raviny character. The accession to the volume of the water in consequence of the junction of these various tributaries leads to an increased width of the sandy bed of the river, but in other respects the character of its banks and low land on the sides remains the same.

At Allahabad the Ganges and Jumna meet and proceed onward in an united stream to the lower provinces. During the rains the enormous body of water which flows down the Ganges swollen by the drainage of the country through which it passes between Hurdwar and Allahabad, impedes the admission of the Jumna, which at this point of junction is dammed up to an extraordinary height, reaching an elevation of 42 feet above the low-water mark of the dry season. Major Rennell, in his memoir, alludes to this circumstance, which has often been doubted, and considered an exaggeration, and I confess that I held some doubts myself on this subject, until I verified the fact in the line of levels taken by me from Cawnpoor to Allahabad in 1844, when I made the most careful observations on the state of the river and the high-water mark as shown by the banks, and as pointed out by the inhabitants of the villages on the spot.

The rivers rise so high on their approach to Allahabad that during the rains they are said to meet at certain points across the Doab, and very heavy embankments and stone dykes are necessary on the Ganges side, on the approach of that river to Allahabad, to prevent accident. The Ganges, down to this point, and on the last 20 miles of its course, is from 2 to 4 miles in width, and inundates a vast tract of country.

Summary of Troughs or K'hadirs.—In looking at the k'hadirs of the Ganges and Jumna from the hills to Allahabad, there are marked peculiarities deserving of attention. The course of the former river is more even, and the river itself runs on a line less tortuous than that of the Jumna. The Ganges, although much depressed below the surface of the high country in its extreme northern regions, runs equably at a depth varying from 70 to 45 feet in its extension to Allahabad. The expanse of k'hadir, looking at the whole line, is tolerably uniform, and the width of the sandy bed upon which the river runs is, in the lower tracts, much in excess to that of the Jumna. The k'hadir of the Jumna, on the contrary, is less depressed at the point where the river leaves the mountains, and onwards towards Panniput, but its width fully equals that of the Ganges. Onwards, however, through the Agra, Etawah, and other districts, the river runs in a deeply excavated and comparatively narrow channel, depressed below the surface of the country to 100 feet and upwards flanked by ravines; and in this respect bears a totally different aspect from that of the Ganges on any part of its course from the hills to Allahabad. Mr. Dodsworth's levels, as shown Pl. vii. Atlas,[1] touch upon the surface level of

[1] Report on the Ganges Canal.

the Jumna in the dry season at eight different points on the left bank, commencing at the junction of the Kurroon Nulla, opposite Agra. They show the following depressions or depths on which the Jumna River runs below the high country lying between the Rinde and the Jumna:—

	Top of bank to surface of Jumna.			Highest land between Rinde and Jumna to surface of Jumna.			Fall of surface of Jumna.	
	Feet	In.		Feet	In.		Feet	In.
Kurroon Junction	72	8·4	......	79	10·0	......	—	—
7 miles lower down	74	8·3	......	81	10·1	......	7	6·9
9 „	72	5·6	......	85	0·0	......	8	6·2
8 „	81	0·9	......	93	9·0	......	12	6·2
5 „	88	0·3	......	96	6·5	......	9	0·9
6 „	85	10·8	......	101	0·0	......	6	3·5
7 „	98	10·8	......	103	11·9	......	14	9·9
6 „	94	0·8	......	102	8·2	......	7	0·47
48 miles.								

This gives a total fall, measuring in straight lines between the points which touched on the Jumna, of 66 ft. 5 in. in 48 miles, or 1·38 feet per mile. The tortuosities of the channel which appear to be marked by the detail of fall above given, would decrease this fall, but it agrees very closely with my observed slope opposite Agra.

At Delhi the Jumna comes in contact with rock, and in the lower part of its course with kunkur beds. The Jumna, in short, has a less uniform k'hadir, than the Ganges, and the extraordinarily tortuous course that it assumes after passing through the Agra and Etawah districts points out in an unmistakeable way the different circumstances, both in bed and slope, under which it reaches Allahabad.

General Description of High Land of the Northern Doab lying between the Ganges and Jumna.—Having in as few words as possible given an outline of the mountains and drainage connected with the Ganges and

Jumna, and described the k'hadirs or low tracts of country through which these rivers run to their junction at Allahabad, I now proceed to bring under review the high land lying between the two rivers; its connection with the rivers themselves; and a topographical outline of the whole surface, bearing upon the irrigation canals that have already been constructed.

The 30th degree of north latitude lies sufficiently close to both the towns of Suharunpoor on the Jumna side, and Hurdwar on the Ganges, to enable me to use that line as a base; the distance of this base from Suharunpoor to Hurdwar is 38 miles, at which point the Ganges leaves the mountains. A perpendicular line, raised from Suharunpoor to a distance of 27 miles touches the point where the Jumna leaves the hills, so that the hypothenuse of the right-angled triangle gives the length of the Sewaliks between the Ganges and the Jumna on their contact with the plains; this length being 46 miles, or thereabouts. The tract of country between the hills and the base before alluded to, lies on a considerable slope on the Jumna side, that from the Kharra head of the Eastern Jumna Canal to Suharunpoor, is not far from 300 feet, and the mountain torrents reach the lines of canal at slopes varying from 5 to 37 feet. The Ganges passes over boulders at Hurdwar, situated on the East of the base line, whilst on the West of the Jumna the bed is sand, the boulder and shingle beds having ceased about 15 to 20 miles above it. The details of the torrents will be entered upon in describing the canal heads; they are chiefly connected with the k'hadir on the flanks, although by artificial cuts from the Muskurra, a portion of the western drainage has been brought to bear upon the West Kalli Nuddi, Hindun and their tributaries.

The Northern Doab, commencing from the 30th

degree of north latitude, terminates in latitude 25° 22″; at the junction of the Ganges and Jumna at Allahabad. Its direction is on a curve bearing to the east. Its length from Suharanpoor to Allahabad is 440 miles, and the maximum and minimum widths, as taken at the following places, are;—

	Miles.		Miles.
Muzuffurnuggur	50	Cawnpoor and Etawah Terminus	35
Bolundshuhur	45	West of Futtipoor	18
Agra and Sikundra Rao	68	East of Futtipoor	25
Futtigurh and Etawah	56	Shahzadpoor	18

These give an average width of about 40 miles.

The drainage of this tract of country is effected by various streams, some of them with troughs or k'hadirs, the character of which, however, is less abrupt than in those of the Ganges and Jumna, the sides being, generally speaking, long, steep, cultivated slopes, even in the early part of their course.

Jumna Drainage described.—The drainage into the Jumna river below the latitude of 30° north, is mainly by the Hindun which enters the Jumna below Delhi; by the Kurroon, which, passing under Sydabad, enters the river just below Agra; and by the Seyngoor and Rinde or Urrund rivers, which join the Jumna near Moosanuggur and Jar-khas, two large towns in the Cawnpoor district.

The Hindun, which rises in the neighbourhood of and above Suharanpoor, was, up to 1825 (at which period cuts were made into its branches for the drainage of the Muskurra river), entirely disconnected from the mountain drainage: its spring heads, are on the Pandooi nulla, at and near the village of Sunkullapoori, not far north of Suharunpoor, and on the Dumola, a branch similarly situated, but draining the country much further north to the eastward of the Pandooi. At Suharunpoor these two streams join, flowing perennially, and ultimately meet the Hindun (which, in two nullas, under the name of the Nugadeo and Gooleria, commences not far from the mountain drainage) at a point near Rusoolpoor and Kujoorwala. The Hindun is then joined by the West Kalli Nuddi, below the town of Boodanuh, after draining a large tract of country extending up to Bhugwanpoor, Roorkee, and the high land that skirts the Ganges k'hadir. South of this the Kirsunni, which rises just below Suharunpoor, with a perennial flow of water, joins the Hindun at the town of Birnawur, and from this point proceeds, without further tributary, to the Jumna through a very extensive k'hadir, carrying in the dry weather a moderate stream of water until it reaches the neighbourhood of Furuknuggur and the suspension bridge at Ghaziooddeennuggur, below which it is only fordable at detached points, with a bad and treacherous bed. It will be seen, therefore, that down to this point the great artery for the drainage on the Jumna watershed, as far south as Delhi, is the Hindun river. There is another minor stream, called the Kattha nulla, which commences in a series of jheels and low country to the east of Rampoor, Kullurpoor, Abba, Teetroon, &c.; this joins the Jumna near Kyrana, 55 miles above Delhi, having passed into the k'hadir at a point about 12 miles north, at the town of Jhinjhanah. The length of the Hindun, measured from its extreme source, is 108 miles; that of the Khatta nulla is 32 miles to its junction with the Jumna. The Kurroon, which rises in the Bolundshuhur district, and the Seyngoor and Rinde, whose heads are not far from each other, situated in a labyrinth of lowland and jheels in the neighbourhood of Alligurh and Sikundra Rao, show that the watershed towards the Jumna and that towards the Ganges is very equally divided; the ridge which separates the actual lines of drainage not being more than 2 or 3 miles in width at the Nugareea and Tureea bridges, on the Ganges Canal; at these points escape channels have been established on the Canal. These three nullas commence in and run through a country with such an entanglement of jheels and hollows, many of the former being of great extent, that it was a very difficult matter to discover the true alignment for the canal channel; this has been done, however, with the greatest care, and with the success that it deserved. As the Seyngoor, Rinde, and Kurroon approach the Jumna, their sections are well defined; they are on that line of their course deep-seated rivers, with (especially in the case of the Seyngoor and Rinde) ravines and broken ground, which, to a person unaccustomed to this species of river, appear almost unaccountable. The lengths of the course of the rivers are as follows:—

Kurroon	80	miles.
Seyngoor	180	,,
Urrund or Rinde . .	200	,,

Ganges Drainage described.—The drainage into the Ganges River, which on 30° N. lat., commences at the debouch of the river from the Sewaliks, is in the upper regions, and to a point about 40 miles south of Hurdwar, entirely by the Solani and its tributaries, which enter the river, having the town of Bhokurheri and the old fort of Sookurtal on the right. The tract of country that provides this drainage is of a very peculiar character, and will be described hereafter when explaining the watershed of the Northern Doab, in connection with the heads of the Ganges and Jumna Canals. At this point it will be sufficient to state that the high bank on which the above towns and fort stand, is on the edge of the Bangur or high land of the Northern Doab.

From the junction of the Solani with the Ganges, down to that of the East Kalli Nuddi, a distance of 225 miles, the high land is entirely drained by this river, which rises north of Meerut at the village of Untwara, and enters the Ganges at Kunnoge, about 32 miles below Futtigurh. The East Kalli Nuddi has, with its tributaries, a length of course equal to 190 miles, or thereabouts, and it is the western boundary of the tract of country which is irrigated by the Futtigurh branch of the Ganges Canal. This river runs through a k'hadir similar to that of the West Kalli Nuddi, and of considerable extent on its approach to the great river. The Eesun, a river 120 miles in length, which rises in the neighbourhood of Sikundra Rao, is a stream of no very great importance, but with extensive lowlands on its whole course. It runs by Mynpoori and enters the Ganges about 18 miles below the junction of the East Kalli Nuddi. Last, as well as least, is the Pandoo, a river with a course of 64 miles, which runs on the West of Cawnpoor, and enters the Ganges about 16 miles below that town.

The watershed of the Northern Doab, therefore, on its eastern face is only relieved by four outlets, its superficial area, as will be seen by the map which accompanies this paper, being of less extent than that on the West.

Description of Works of Irrigation.—The whole extent of the high land, with the two great rivers that border it on its right and left flank, having now been described thus summarily, I will proceed to an account of the works for irrigation that have been executed, entering into more detail on actual levels, and the bearing of the high upon the low land, than I have hitherto done.

In carrying out the works both of the Ganges and Jumna Canals, the great object has been to keep the channel on the ridge separating the watersheds. Even on the Eastern Jumna Canal, the direction of which was projected by native engineers, it is curious to observe how accurately this has been effected; for although, to save expense, they took possession of hollows, and even a line of drainage called the Shamli nulla, the general position is admirably adapted for throwing water over the neighbouring country. On the Ganges Canal the ridge has been occupied in its fullest extent, the most elevated points in a series of cross sections of the country having been taken possession of; the direction of the courses of the different rivers, and the position of the Ganges Canal with reference to them and to their heads, as shown by the map, will fully verify this assertion.

Sanitary considerations, founded upon the experience of grave events, pointed out the necessity of avoiding the proximity of large towns and military cantonments, and especially cautioned us against the evils of intercepting the natural drainage of the country. One of the great advantages, in fact, of the line as passing through the Meerut district was that it altogether avoided the town and cantonment of Meerut, which it left at a distance of eight miles off. With the exception of Cawnpoor at the terminus of the Canal on the Ganges, it will be observed, by reference to the map, that towns and cantonments are passed at a considerable distance. I am now writing of matters as they existed at the close of the year 1839, when my first survey of the main line commenced. Roorkee was at that time a mere village; it is now a town, with extensive cantonments, both civil and military; but even at that time, which was long antecedent to the medical inquiries as to the effect of irrigation canals on the sanitary state of the country, my own experience led me not only to avoid towns and cantonments, but to look upon the intersection of nullas and rivers, and consequent interference with the natural drainage of the country, as not admissible. These are points worthy of consideration, as if they are *not* to be considered, and if an engineer is allowed to treat with indifference evils of the greatest magnitude, and to throw on one side rules by which my operations were guided—to act, in short, in opposition to all rules—he has a great advantage over me, and may, much to his own satisfaction, no doubt, give *ex cathedrâ* opinions on the fundamental mistakes with which he charges me.

Here I may advert to the object of the Ganges Canal as designed by me. This object was to give irrigation to all the districts from Suharunpoor downwards to Cawnpoor, and to use the Ganges water in irrigating the k'hadir or tract lying between Hurdwar and Roorkee, when water could be spared for such a purpose. On this point, I observe in my report:—" From the uncertainty " that exists as to the amount of water which will be " taken for irrigation in the k'hadir, and the means that " (from its proximity to the Ganges River) we have of " restoring any quantity of water that may be so taken, " without interfering with the calculated supply for the " lower regions, we may consider that at Roorkee, where " the canal touches the high land, the supply of water is " equal to 6,750 cubic feet per second." —(Vol. I., p. 191, Ganges Canal Report.)

In addition to the irrigation of the different districts through which it passed, the water power introduced by the falls was adapted to machinery for corn mills, and lockage was given at all the falls so that the line might be passable for boats and rafts. Irrigation, however, was obviously the object of this work: its very history points out this.

Originating in the Guntoor famine, and under the auspices of Mr. Thomason, a Lieutenant-Governor, whose views were entirely devoted to land revenue, and whose every thought was in making Canals for Irrigation, not only to produce plenty in the districts through which they passed, but to be accessories to railroads in furnishing the means of distributing plenty elsewhere, navigation was a secondary object entirely. It is, in fact, doubtful how far irrigation and navigation can be carried on conjointly without the one clashing with the interests of the other. So far as my experience goes, there are years (and by no means of unfrequent occurrence), when the country is visited by drought, during which no amount of superintendence could protect the watercourse heads from the cultivators, so as to maintain navigation in an irrigation canal.[1]

Where water is so plentiful, and where irrigation is so little demanded, that the engineer can afford to raise the flooring of the watercourse heads above the bed of the canal, and thereby maintain a depth of water in the canal channel sufficient and solely for the purposes of navigation, navigation will of course be secured. This however is not the case in the North-Western Provinces: every drop of water that can be obtained is required and used for agricultural purposes.

At page 309, vol. II., of my Ganges Canal report, I give my reasons for not carrying the channel for naviga-

[1] During heavy droughts, I have known the tail of the Main Trunk of both the Eastern and Western Jumna Canals to be frequently dry. I recollect during one season that on the most urgent application from me to the Superintendent of the Western Jumna Canals to keep, at any rate, the Ellenborough tank in the city of Delhi filled with water, he was positively unable to do so.

tion in one consecutive line instead of confining it to each individual fall. The chief reason was expense (the reason, in fact, which deterred me from using stone where stone would have been so desirable); but the advantage of a line for boats parallel to and entirely independent of the main channel would be exceedingly great, and might, in all probability, be kept more efficient and be less interrupted than the channel is in its present form. From Roorkee, therefore, or from the head of the Asoffnuggur Falls, a navigable line, carried parallel to and separate from the main canal, might be of great value. In the North-Western Provinces water is the manure of the land, and its application to agriculture is of infinite importance. The principle on which the Canals in these Provinces have been projected appears to me to be in every way the best adapted to their wants: viz., that the water should be at the disposal of the agriculturist, and that navigation should be entirely subservient to his interests; that is to say, so long as there is water running in the Canal sufficient for the passage of boats, boats may be used upon it; when the fields require the water for irrigation, the passage of boats must cease.

Eastern and Western Jumna Canals described.—In giving a description of the Canals in the Northern Doab, I cannot do better than transcribe from vol. I., p. 107, *et sequitur*, of my Ganges Canal report, the topographical features of the country through which the Jumna Canals pass. In tracing on the map the direction of the Jumna from the point where it leaves the Hills to Delhi, and observing the position of the Eastern and Western Jumna Canals, with their heads of supply opposite to each other, their alignments parallel, and their escape or tail water joining the parent stream at points also opposite, an indifferent observer would naturally conclude that under circumstances so strikingly coincident, such difficulties as were due to surface contour would be common to both, and that the works required for the maintenance of one canal would, *cæteris paribus*, be similar to those of the other.

In the central and southern regions the levels of both Canals correspond in a general way. On the eastern bank, however, the limit of the river valley or k'hadir is thrown back as far as the village of Surrowli on the Eastern Jumna Canal, a distance of about 12 miles from the existing bed of the stream, and the step thereby caused is passed by a succession of falls and lockage. On the western bank, the high land bounding the k'hadir is maintained up to the immediate vicinity of the city of Delhi, to which the Western Jumna Canal is enabled to provide an abundant supply of water for domestic use. The rapid descent into the valley of the river takes place virtually at the tail of the canal, and the fall thus obtained is economized for flour mills, worked by the surplus water, for which an escape into the river is provided through paved and well-protected channels.

It is in the northern region where we observe the greatest difference. On the West of the Jumna, the canal on leaving the parent stream passes over wide and open beds of shingle, upon which the force of the stream is able to exhaust itself: these beds extend as far south as the latitude of the Dadoopoor dam, a distance of 16 miles, and during the whole of their course are the recipients of the country drainage, which passes off during floods either over the country, or through breaches, which are repaired annually after the rainy months. The Dadoopoor dam, which regulates the supply into the Canal channel, is also the escape of the flood water of the Putralla and Sombe, across the united channels of which the dam is built, the latter being a torrent of very large dimensions. From the dam the canal proceeds along the low land, or k'hadir, until it reaches a point 60 miles below Dadoopoor, at which it has gained the levels of the high country, continuing to follow these to Delhi on its left, and Hansi on its right branch.

Although, therefore, masonry works are provided on this Canal for the passage of the Putralla and Sombe torrents, the two following facts render the occurrence of floods, even of an extraordinary volume, a matter of comparatively little moment:—viz., first, that 60 miles of its course are in the k'hadir, or low lands of the Jumna, through which the channel wanders with all the tortuosity of a natural river; and, secondly, that the whole line, after its escape from the shingle beds, is out of the influence of the rapid slopes, which are natural to the proximity of the mountains. Leaving out of the question the Putralla and Sombe, floods do, in fact, pass directly over the course of this canal on the tracts, above and below Dadoopoor, without doing any material injury either to the works or to the country.

The Eastern Jumna Canal, after passing down the shingly bed of the Boodhee Jumna, for the short distance of 4 miles, enters on deep cutting, and takes a south-easterly direction, commencing at the village of Nyashur; from this point it plunges at once into all the difficulties peculiar to a line crossing mountain drainage at right angles to its course; the Raipoor, Jatonwala, Nogong, and Muskurra, four mountain torrents of greater or less dimensions, are passed within a distance of 10 miles from the Nyashur deep cutting. The Muskurra and the Nogong are torrents of considerable magnitude, and are provided with masonry dams for floods during rains. After crossing the Muskurra, the Eastern Jumna Canal channel continues on the high land of the country.

With a similar declivity, therefore, on both the

Eastern and Western Jumna Canals, between their terminal points, the distribution in detail leads to most remarkable differences in the requirements for works. The great northern step, which on the Western Canal is passed by a succession of wide beds of shingle, with considerable tortuosity of channel, through low or k'hadir country, is on the Eastern line maintained for many miles on the high lands in the face of numerous mountain torrents, and finally overcome by a succession of masonry falls. These characteristic differences, accordingly, determine the nature of the means to be employed in passing this step of country. On the West, the broad and winding beds of shingle absorb the fall naturally and easily, and thus obviate the necessity of artificial descents. On the East, where no such low shingly tracts are to be met with, but where the Canal at once enters the high land of the country, the common object must be attained by purely artificial and expensive falls.

Both these canals derive their supply of water from the Jumna, at points where the bed consists of boulders and shingle, where its slope is very great, and where, in consequence, spurs thrown out into the main stream direct the water into the mouth of the excavated channel of the Canal head with facility, and under great advantages. When, as it occasionally happens in years, when the demand for water for irrigation is extensive, the spurs are projected right across the Jumna so as to form a temporary dam; this great slope of bed relieves the dam from excessive head water, and its concomitant evils. The process is an exceedingly simple one, and if the excavated channel to admit the Canal supply be carried to a sufficient depth, and made of sufficient capacity, there is no reason why the whole of the river might not be thrown down the cut at a very moderate expense. There *is* difficulty, no doubt, in maintaining the heads and spurs in the face of the sudden rises of the river; and during the rains, the floods throw banks of shingle over the head of the cut, which have to be removed to admit of the cold weather supply. Nevertheless, with the comparatively small bodies of water which we have to deal with, the supply of the Jumna Canal has been maintained without any extraordinary difficulty, and without any necessity for permanent works. It will be understood that the boulders in the bed of the river, and the jungly nature of the country in the vicinity of these heads, afford ample material for the execution of the works, whilst the water, which during a great portion of the year is fresh from the mountains, passes into the canal heads free from silt and impurities.

The appended sketches will show in detail the Jumna and its branches as connected with the heads of the Eastern and Western Jumna Canals, Plates 4 and 5; these, with the general map which is given as a frontispiece to this paper, will, I believe, elucidate the subject as far as is necessary for my purpose.

We must now inquire as to the possibility of obtaining the supply for these Canals from points on the Jumna below their shingly tracts, by establishing dams across the river in positions removed from the mountain torrents, and consequently at points in its course where the low land, or k'hadir, is very extensive, and where the bed of the river itself is sand.

I commence with the Western Jumna Canal, which runs for a distance of 60 miles from the head down the k'hadir of the Jumna to a point 6 miles below Kurnal. Here the canal enters the *Bangur* or high land of the country, after having overcome the steep slope by meandering through the natural channels of boulders and shingle, which constitute the early part of its course.

From what has been said before, it will not be difficult to understand that the canal in the vicinity of Kurnal is very little, if at all, elevated above the Jumna itself; in fact, the levels taken from the Jumna not far above Kurnal were found to be so favourable to a head of supply, that a point was selected for that purpose near the village of Kulsowra, where the river approaches the canal to within a distance of 6 miles or thereabouts, and where the width of the k'hadir, on the right of the river, is somewhat contracted.

The whole of a working season, that is to say, the period from the close of the rains in 1827, to the commencement of the rains in 1828 (from November in one year to May in the other), was occupied in driving piles and forming other protective works for a new head; and arrangements were made at considerable expense for preserving the work that was done, or partly so, from the effects of the floods of the forthcoming season. These, however, were of no avail; the whole was swept away, and, as far as my recollection goes, not a vestige of the works was left. What the engineer's ultimate intentions were, whether to establish a head with temporary bunds and spurs, or whether to throw a dam across the channel, I am quite unable to say; but I am satisfied of this, that whatever was done, was well digested and well planned, and was not a mere[1] nothing, as Sir Arthur Cotton, in his unbounded presumption, is pleased to assert.

The results of this trial were so unfortunate, and they so completely verified the prognostications of the people who were acquainted with the rise and fall, and the fierce action of the flood water on the alluvial soil, that nothing further was attempted. This happened in

[1] "Probably this attempt, was the merest nothing." *See* p. 84, of Sir A. Cotton's Pamphlet.

1828. The Ganges Canal works were brought under consideration in 1836, only eight years later. Is it by any means wonderful that the ill-success of the Kulsowra works should have had some effect in warning the engineers to avoid any attempt at taking a head from the sandy tracts of the Ganges? Is it at all extraordinary that I should have recorded this, as the last experiment that was made, no other canal in the North-Western Provinces, up to the period of the survey of the Ganges Canal, having been projected? Yet this statement made by me is treated in Sir A. Cotton's usual fashion. "Suppose men were to argue now, because men did not "know how to construct first-class railways *thirty-six* "*years ago*, therefore they could not be made *now*—the "case is precisely the same." *See* p. 84. Again, "If "we are to act upon the failures of thirty-six years "ago, rather than by the successes achieved since, "we must not only give up these anicuts and railways, "but also ocean steam navigation, Enfield rifles, the "overland route," &c. (*See* p. 85 of Sir A. Cotton's pamphlet.) Whatever strides may have been made in Europe in the application of raw material in the arts and sciences, whether for locomotion, or for fixed machinery, or for any other purpose, none have been made in connection with throwing dams over the great rivers running in *alluvial troughs* in India. The dams built by Sir A. Cotton are merely an extension (for which he deserves the highest credit) of a system practised centuries before in the Madras Presidency, and although he may have been successful with the rivers that he has had to deal with, it by no means follows that the deductions we have arrived at from observation, and the experiments which have led us to our conclusions are wrong, or that in dealing with the Ganges and Jumna flowing in *deep troughs* at the foot of the

Himalaya, we should be as successful as he has been with the Kistna and Godaveri Rivers running in their *Deltaic segments* above the surface of the country on their approach to the ocean.

I honestly confess that, in 1836, I looked upon dams constructed across the sandy k'hadirs as entirely out of the question. In 1864, twenty-eight years later, I am still of the same opinion, and feel satisfied that were Sir A. Cotton to attempt to throw one of his dams, constructed on the Madras principle, across either the Ganges or Jumna at points below the shingle, it would suffer the fate of the works at Kulsowra, and, as I have expressed myself before, "the works would be breached, "and washed away on the occurrence of the first "flood."

The neighbourhood of Kurnal was the only site below the shingly tracts adapted for a head for the Western Jumna Canals; the great extent of the k'hadir above, and the nature of its surface, rendered any position higher up, on the course of the river, dangerous.

To construct a dam with a waste-board permanently elevated to a great height, or even to any height at all, across the Jumna, where the low land that would come under the influence of inundation is from 10 to 12 miles wide, with a portion only elevated above flood water height, would be destructive. It must be recollected, moreover, that as the canal revenue at the time to which we refer was 2½ laks of rupees, and as now it is only 4 laks, financial reasons might have intervened to prevent such a work from being done effectively.

We must now turn our attention to the opposite side of the river and to the Eastern Jumna Canal, which has none of the advantages of the Western in having escaped artificial works, by the expenditure of fall of country over beds of shingle. The Eastern Jumna Canal strikes off from the shingle beds to the high land at a point distant only 3 or 4 miles from the Kharra Head, and passes with a very heavy fall across the drainage of the mountains, until it reaches the open country of the Doab at Kulsea on the left bank of the Muskurra torrent. Why should not a dam have been built across the Jumna below, instead of proceeding to Fyzabad and the higher region at the Kharra Head? An inspection of the map with a moderate understanding of the contour of the country will, I think, show that in this case, the engineer had no choice. The alternative would have been in a cut from the Jumna meeting the line of canal at some point between Kulsea and Suharunpoor, perhaps below the falls at Ghoonna. Now, since this cut would not have avoided any of the mountain torrents that cross the line as it at present runs, it would have met them under more difficult circumstances, and after their entrance into the low land. The site of the dam in the Jumna would have been in the latitude of the town of Behut or that of the village of Kulsea, and the line from the dam would have run obliquely across the k'hadir, probably between Putehur and Sooltanpoor Chilkhana. The k'hadir here is 10 or 12 miles in width, and from the nature of the drainage across it, utterly unadapted to works of any sort. This may be said of all this k'hadir, from the canal head downwards. This canal gives a return in gross revenue of 2¾ laks of rupees; and as in the case of the Western Jumna Canals, it might be doubtful whether, in an economical point of view, the construction, or rather, I should say, the attempt at construction of such a work, as a dam in the Great River, would be warranted.

It is useless and unprofitable to discuss this question further. It does not apply to the comparatively small canals on the Jumna so much as it does to the Ganges Canal, where the works necessary to pass the k'hadir are on such a large scale, although the amount of descent on the Eastern Jumna Canal before reaching the irrigating districts is equally great.

To talk of experiments is to presuppose that the cost of a dam has been estimated and sanctioned; a consummation not at all likely to take place. It is only, I imagine, by actual attempt at construction that, in the diametrically opposite views taken on the subject by Sir Arthur Cotton and myself, the question at issue can be determined. He, no doubt, (judging from the tone of his pamphlet), considers that I am as ignorant and without experience, as I am persuaded that his estimates are worthless and his schemes visionary. I am quite content to let the matter rest in this position, until it shall have been practically decided by experiment.

In my reply to Sir Arthur Cotton's asserted fourth fundamental mistake of my project, where he draws a comparison between the dams on the Godaveri and Kistna, and the very minor work, as he considers it, which must be constructed at the Ganges Canal head above Hurdwar, I write as follows:—

" The question, however, of throwing a permanent " dam or anicut across the Ganges at the point desired, " is by no means so simple as Sir Arthur Cotton imagines. " His experience, great as it is, is connected with rivers " of an entirely different description from that of the " Ganges in its debouch from the Sewaliks. Here " we have heavy slopes with large masses of water " pouring down with overwhelming violence; there he " has much larger bodies of water, but on very much " smaller slopes in connection with a true Delta. Sir " Arthur Cotton gives the following statement of dis- " charges:—

	Cubic Yards per Hour.
" Ganges	25,000,000
" Godaveri	200,000,000
" Kistna	160,000,000 "[1]

the question being confined to the above three rivers.

Sir Arthur Cotton's professional reputation is derived from his treatment of rivers in their Deltaic segments, which bear the character that I have above given them; they run on comparatively low slopes with large bodies of water. "*It appears to be possible* " *to secure foundations on the rivers of Southern India* " *with their very low slopes, &c.,*" says the late Colonel Baird Smith; and no doubt the general character of these rivers is of that description. Sir Arthur Cotton refers me to the Pallaur Anicut, where, as he states, the fall is 10 feet a mile and the bed is of sand, as a proof of his experience of rivers with sandy beds and heavy slopes. It is not clear how this dam is situated, nor under what circumstances it receives floods; but at any rate, it appears to be an exceptional case, and, as such, by no means disproves my assertion "that " his experience, great as it is, is connected with rivers of " an entirely different description from that of the Ganges " in its debouch from the Sewaliks, &c. &c." The three great rivers with which his name is connected have slopes of bed as follows:—

Cauveri	3½ feet per mile.[2]
Kistna	12 inches per mile.
Godaveri	5 inches per mile.

[1] I cite the above, although by no means satisfied of the correctness of the figures.

[2] Colonel Baird Smith notes on this:—" Strangely enough I have " not been able to find on record a single longitudinal section of the " beds, either of the main stream or of the branches. The distribution " of slope is, therefore, not so precisely known as it ought to be; but " I learn that the fall of the bed of the main stream at the point of

At p. 82 of Sir Arthur Cotton's pamphlet, in replying to my statement, he writes: "A great portion of the "reply I am now remarking upon, is based on this *en-* "*tirely imaginary ground*, that weirs *cannot be built across a* "*river having a bed of sand.* In all my communications "with the officers connected with the canal, the line of "argument runs, in fact, thus:—*We have never built* "*weirs across large rivers with sandy beds, therefore they* "*never can be built*," and so on.

No engineer connected with the canal department in the North-West Provinces can possibly have asserted that weirs cannot be built across a river with a sandy bed.

From the very circumstance of the supply of these canals being taken from points high up in the Jumna and Ganges, the canals themselves are in contact with numerous mountain torrents, which cross them at right angles, and force upon the engineer the construction of dams and weirs over *beds of sand* of unlimited depths. These dams and weirs are, in fact, *the* difficulties of the North-Western Provinces' engineer. See the dams on the Muskurra, Nogong, and Rutmoo, on slopes of bed, 9½ feet, 11½ and 8 feet per mile respectively. See, also, the dam over the united torrents of the Putrala and Sombe on the Western Jumna Canal. Sir Arthur Cotton has, I apprehend, misunderstood the expressions of "the officers "connected with the canal," who referred to the great trough rivers, the Ganges and Jumna.

To continue my description of the watershed of the

"separation is 3½ feet per mile; that this slope is continued for a con- "siderable distance down the Coleroon branch, gradually lessening "however, so that 70 miles below the head of Seringham it has fallen "to 2 feet per mile, while onward to the sea this average slope may be "estimated at 1 foot per mile; and that further the general fall of the "Cauveri Branch is about 4½ or 5 inches less per mile than that of the "Coleroon."—*Cauveri, Kistna and Godavery*, BAIRD SMITH, p. 9.

Northern Doab as connected with the canals at the foot of the Sewaliks:—

Drainage of the Eastern Jumna Canal or Western watershed.—One very remarkable feature in the topography of the country over which the Eastern Jumna Canal passes, will give at once a key to the general remedies that were at hand for enabling us to contend against the difficulties due to the torrents which crossed the line in its passage onwards from Nyashur; and as these were remedies which are not always to be found when projecting canal alignments, they are worthy of record here.

From the description before given of the direction taken by the Eastern Jumna Canal on its leaving the parent stream, and entering upon the high land at Nyashur, it will be observed that the very circumstance of the line of canal running at right angles to the drainage of the mountains, and, consequently, in a direction parallel to these mountains, showed that the country sloped from west to east, and, therefore, that, although the mountain drainage in its natural state crossed the canal line, we held the power in our hands of changing the course of the drainage at points lying above the canal channel, and by passing the water off to the eastward, of relieving the works from a great deal of the inconvenience to which they were naturally subjected.

A leading feature in the original project was the neutralization of the effects of the Muskurra upon the works at Kulsea by taking advantage of this natural arrangement of slopes and by turning its waters to the eastward; to connect them at three different points with rivers which were tributary to the Hindun. The effect of these arrangements has been to reduce the Muskurra at its point of contact with the masonry dam at Kulsea to a comparatively inconsiderable volume. The Jatonwala drainage has on the same principle been turned into the Nogong river. At times the violence of the Nogong flood has been relieved by allowing a portion of its volume to pass down the canal channel towards the Muskurra. The influence of the arrangement of surface slope above described has therefore been undoubtedly of the highest importance and value to the works on the Eastern Jumna Canal.

Drainage at the head of the Ganges Canal or Eastern watershed.—It is with the above peculiarities of drainage as affecting the works in the northern district of the Eastern Jumna Canal, which is in itself in fact the western watershed of the Northern Doab, and with the details of this tract of country fresh in recollection, that I would turn the reader's attention to the Eastern watershed, or the drainage which flows into the Ganges river. The line of separation is well defined: the Western drainage, including the West Kalli Nuddi and its tributaries, flows into the Jumna; the Eastern, including the East Kalli Nuddi and its tributaries, flows into the Ganges: the point of separation in the Sewaliks being the Shahjuhanpoor and Koojnawur Passes, to reach which from the plains, a section of country free from cross-drainage, is traversed; this section being in fact the backbone of the Doab.

It will be observed, by referring to the map, that from the point of watershed, or from that ravine in the hills which supplies the most westerly tributary of the Solani river, there is a bank which extends in a south-easterly direction, increasing in departure from the hills as it proceeds onwards: upon the edge of this bank are situated the towns of Bhugwanpoor, Roorkee, Jourassi, Lundhoura, Noornuggur, and on and near its approach to the main stream of the river Ganges, the towns of

Bhokurheeri and the old fort at Sookurtal. These towns overlook, as it were, an extensive valley, the depression of which under Noornuggur is 80 feet, and that at Kumbhera, a village situated 7 miles lower down on the crest of the bank, is 82½ feet, to the bed of the Bhat Nuddi; to the surface of the water in the old Ganges at the village of Badshahpoor it is 83¼ feet. In other words, at the village of Kumbhera, which is situated 10 miles above the fort at Sookurtal, the crest of this bank is 82½ and 83¼ feet above the valley below it. The tract of country referred to, bounded by the Sewaliks and the high bank above described, receives the whole of the hill drainage from the western extremity of the watershed; this drainage is, in fact, restricted to the above limits by a well-defined barrier. To the West of the high bank the drainage of the country passes off by shallow tributaries to the West Kalli Nuddi, and ultimately to the Jumna river. Sand-hills (provincially termed *B'hoor*) are here a remarkable feature; these show themselves in undulating elevations and depressions running parallel to the drainage of the West Kalli Nuddi; sometimes, however, they are found in ramifications, thrown off from the main line, pierced at points to admit of the passage of the side drainage; occasionally, in extended and in broken ridges. The slope of the country is from the edge of this high bank towards the west, and strange as it may appear,[1] the watershed line of the Jumna and Ganges passes directly along the top of the ridge on which the towns are situated.

[1] Colonel W. E. Baker, R.E., informs me that the water-shed line of the Sutlej and Jumna runs across the parade at Kurnal, close upon the edge of the Jumna k'hadir. The tendency of slope towards the Sutlej is shown also by the direction given to the Hansi canal. See Plate 1, frontispiece.

The low tract of country which I have before described is that portion of the Ganges k'hadir with which the works on the Ganges Canal are connected. It is of a triangular form bounded on the north-east by the Sewalik hills, on the south-west and south by a bank, and on the south and east by the Ganges river. The Sewaliks on the north-east, and the bank which lies on the south-west and south meet at an acute angle near the Shahjuhanpoor and Koojnawur Passes; the bank, decreasing in abruptness up to this point of junction, in the vicinity of which it is lost entirely. The k'hadir receives the whole of the drainage up to this angle, which is the true point of departure of the watershed separating the drainage of the Jumna and Ganges rivers. The depression of the triangle thus defined, is by no means uniform; to the westward there is an isolated portion considerably elevated, on which are situated the towns of Kheri, Imli, and numerous villages; the surface of this elevated portion is much intersected by channels, and it is separated, or nearly so, in its centre by a large ravine receiving a portion of the drainage collected in the forests. In addition to this main insular tract of high land, there are other smaller mounds in detached or outlying positions upon which villages have been built. The town or village of Dowlutpoor is thus situated, and to the north of Dowlutpoor the mounds or knolls appear to be ramifications from the higher levels lying at the foot of the hills, above which they are much elevated. The drainage is well marked, and may be divided into three distinct basins, the most westerly one embracing all the hills and country lying to the north of Kheri and Shah Munsoor, including the drainage from mountain torrents on a distance of 8 miles from the western angle: this, which is by far the most extensive, has its waters collected into the Solani river which flows at the base of the high bank, and after receiving tributaries from the greater part of the k'hadir, reaches the Ganges in the neighbourhood of Bhokurheri. The Ganges Canal passes the Solani on an aqueduct, the flooring of which is 24 feet above the bed of the river—the water-way for the river is 750 wide in 15 bays of 50 feet each, and the water-way of the masonry aqueduct for the passage of the canal water is 170 feet.

The second, or central basin is drained by the Rutmoo river, the heads of which are in the neighbourhood of Shah Munsoor. This river receives the water falling on a width of 11 miles of mountain, and is a tributary of the Solani, which it joins under the town of Jourassi. The Ganges Canal passes the Rutmoo, their beds being on the same level, and the water being retained by a masonry dam.

The third is the Puttri basin, which receives all the water from the country between the towns of Gur'h and Jowallapoor, with a hill drainage 6 miles in width. The drainage of the Puttri, however, is in the earlier parts of its course divided into two distinct mountain torrents, the one to the westward being *par excellence* the Puttri; that to the eastward, and in the neighbourhood of Jowallapoor, being called the Ranipoor Rao. These two branches, as they may be designated, run in separate, though ill defined basins, being to all intents and purposes, distinct torrents, and as such have been separately treated. The Ganges Canal passes *under* both these torrents, for which super-passages are provided of 300 and 200 feet in width respectively.

To the eastward of the Puttri drainage, or rather to the eastward of that drainage connected with the Ranipoor river, and the town of Hurdwar, where the Sewalik hills impinge upon the Ganges river, there is a good deal of scattered drainage, which during heavy rains comes down with great rapidity from the low spurs and ridges which lie at the foot of the Sewaliks; the water derived from this source passes directly into the Ganges, through numerous small channels which lie to the south of Hurdwar and Kunkhul.

The Solani and Rutmoo rivers exhibit in their course under the bank at Bhugwanpoor and Roorkee, unmistakeable marks of their mountain origin; they are Raos,[1] in the most extended sense, with wide sandy beds, and although during exceedingly dry seasons showing no external stream, they bear under a dry sandy surface perennial spring water.

The Puttri and Ranipoor differ very materially from those above described. In the proximity of the hills they exhibit the character of mountain torrents, with shingle and sand in a well defined bed; this condition terminates a few miles from the mountains in wide expanses of sand, which are thrown over the country, leading to the entire disappearance of channel or bed, the sand being frequently cultivated. At lower levels and further down the valley, well marked sections again present themselves, at detached points only, scattered here and there over the surface of the country. In a more southerly direction these detached bits of drainage become united in one perfect channel, which skirting the Puttri forest, wanders ultimately over the low lands, and joins

1 Rao (Torrent) a provincial name given to the shallow, sandy, or shingle beds directly connected with the Hills, the drainage of which is carried off by their channels. During the greater portion of the year they are either perfectly dry, or with a small stream running in them. After heavy rain they are liable to severe freshes and floods, and at this time are impassable for man or beast. The great declivity upon which they run, enables them to pour out a volume of water with immense and dangerous velocity. These floods, however, do not last above a few hours, and subside as rapidly as they commenced.

the labyrinth of rivers which intersect the k'hadir at its south-eastern extremity.

In further illustration of the features of this tract of k'hadir, I may observe that although spring water may be, and is even at the hottest periods of the year found near the surface in the immediate vicinity of the hills, it is one of the characteristic phenomena here as elsewhere, on the line of country lying at the foot of the Sewaliks (as I have before observed) that on a belt extending to an irregular width south of, and parallel to the hills, water is only found at considerable depths, whereas at points lying beyond this belt, spring water either appears at the surface, or can be obtained by very moderate excavations. In exemplification of the above, it was found that in all our excavations lying at a moderate distance from the foot of the hills, neither spring water, nor any appearance of spring water exhibited itself. As we got further from the hills, and arrived at the Puttri works, where we had to carry the excavation to great depths, we came upon spring water at a depth of 7¼ feet below the surface. The Badshahpoor Nulla, with which we came in contact between the Puttri and Rutmoo valley, was, in fact, an open perennial stream. The ridge between the Rutmoo and the Solani river was by no means free from an inconvenience of this nature, which we did not get rid of until we reached the excavation on the high land of Roorkee.

With the exception of the tract in the immediate neighbourhood of the towns of Kunkhul, Hurdwar, and other villages scattered at detached points along the foot of the hills, the whole of the country lying at the foot of the Sewaliks, and at the heads of the torrents above described, was at the period of my commencing the survey of this portion of the k'hadir in 1839, forest and uncultivated; and although the triangular tract which I have described under the name of the k'hadir, was neither wanting in villages nor population, the greater portion of it was jungle and marsh; of the latter there were some very extensive tracts connected with the Puttri, situated centrically, and to the eastward of Santuh Shah; and others, with the Solani and B'hat rivers, which under the name of the Jogiwalla-jheel, covered a large area of country near Bhokurheri, were, at the time of which I talk, supposed to be, in their innermost recesses, inaccessible.

Advantages of taking Heads from Shingle tracts above Hurdwar.—Having thus entered into a full description of the heads of both the canals on the Jumna, and shown the necessity for drawing their supplies from the shingle tracts under the mountains—instead of from the sandy beds of the river at points lower down in its course—and having described the watershed of the country lying at the foot of the hills both on the East and West as connected with the great rivers, I now proceed to the head of the Ganges Canal, taken off under similar circumstances from the Ganges river, at a point where the bed is shingly, and where the slope is great; and I intend not only to show how obviously advantageous it was in every point of view to select this particular spot as the site of the canal head, but how impracticable it would have been to have gained the required object otherwise.

Before entering upon this subject, however, there must be no misunderstanding on two points :—

1st. With the rapid slope of the surface of the country from Sookurtal downwards, and the comparatively low slope of the bed of the Ganges river running parallel, nobody ever doubted that the levels were adapted to making a canal, or so far as *they* alone were concerned, that *they* offered any impediment.

2nd. When asserting, that a dam raised 10 or 15 feet above the surface of low-water mark in the Ganges river *cannot* be built at a point near or below Sookurtal, with the slightest chance of its withstanding the effect of floods, my meaning must be taken in an economic sense. With unlimited outlay a dam might be built across the Ganges sufficient for any purpose.

The direction of the canal as projected by me will be understood from the map, frontispiece, Plate 1; and the details of the bed of the Ganges, whence the head supply is taken off above Hurdwar, will be understood by Plate 3.

The plan adopted here for taking off the supply was precisely the same as that on the Jumna, which I have before described. The difficulties were greater, as it may be understood from the larger body of water required for the canal, and from the greater capacity of channel necessary to admit the supply. The remarks on the Jumna Heads, however, apply equally, in so far that the slope of the cut not being so rapid nor so abrupt as that of the main river, vast accumulations of shingle are, during floods in the rainy season, thrown over the mouth, the removal of which, together with the reconstruction or repair of the spurs and bunds in the main channel, is of much greater detriment to the early supply, and to the efficient maintenance of their heads, than those of a similar character (although smaller in extent) are on the Jumna.

The experience of 10 years has, so far as I can discover, amply proved this; and the observations of Colonel Baird Smith, as recorded in his Famine Report, p. 66, par. 126, leave no doubt in my mind that measures ought to be taken to secure a permanent head by a weir over the main Ganges. A bar or weir, *of no great elevation*, extending right across the bed of the river, is all that is required. This, although costly, will be, comparatively speaking, easily built, from the nature of the boulder bed in which the foundations will be laid, and from the proximity of boulders and heavy material for the superstructure.

The difficulties that I had to contend against in the passage of the numerous torrents referred to in my description of the k'hadir, and the great expense incurred in their construction, would of course have been all avoided by the simple expedient of damming the Ganges at Sookurtal, and we now have to inquire whether, in an economic point of view, such would have been advisable.

The levels of the surface of the backbone or ridge of the high country from Roorkee to Cawnpoor and Allahabad are as follows:

On the 1st 20 miles from Roorkee to Bailra a fall of 46 ft., or 2·3 ft. pr mile.

„	2nd 20	miles	a fall of	32	feet or	1·6	feet per mile.
„	3rd 20	„	„	29·5	„	1·47	„
„	4th 20	„	„	35	„	1·75	„
„	5th 20	„	„	33·34	„	1·66	„
„	6th 20	„	„	28·5	„	1·42	„
„	7th 20	„	„	27·73	„	1·38	„
„	8th 20	„	„	26·86	„	1·34	„

From Nanoon to Cawnpoor 169 miles a fall of 189 ft., or 1·11 ft. per mile.
From Cawnpoor to Allahabad 113 miles a fall of 101 feet 1·1 in. or 10·78 feet per mile.

The levels of the cold weather surface of the Ganges cannot be given in such great detail, but we may gather from the surveys the true levels of the surface at Gurmukhtesur Ghat, and thence to a point about 180 miles lower down the stream, and 35 miles below Futtigurh, after which we come in contact with the river again at Cawnpoor, and finally near the junction of the Ganges and Jumna at Allahabad; so that we have a close approximation to the slopes of the surface of the Ganges river from the Gurmukhtesur Ghat to Allahabad.

Above Gurmukhtesur Ghat to Sookurtal I have no levels of the river, and, as is shown in page 8 of my pamphlet, I have been necessitated to introduce an hypothetical level reduced from other surveys, and based on the supposition that the fall between an old branch of the Ganges at Badshahpoor and the surface of the main river at Sookurtal was 1·25 feet per mile.

The total fall from the top of the high bank at Kumbhera, which is described as 84 feet above the level of the branch of the Ganges at Badshahpoor, to the top of the high land at Bhokurheri, in a distance of 7 miles, is 14·78 feet, and 3 miles further, in the vicinity of Sookurtal, the fall is 6·92 feet; the fall, therefore, on the top of the bank is upwards of 2 feet per mile. Hence, I believe, that considering the position of the Badshahpoor branch, and its distance from Sookurtal; the fact that the surface of the water in those branches which are more or less dammed up, is usually higher than the parent stream at an opposite point; and the above circumstance of the fall on the top of the bank; that the true slope between Badshahpoor and Sookurtal would be nearer 2 feet than 1·25 feet.

Leaving this as a doubtful question, we will consider the levels of the surface of the water in the cold weather at Gurmukhtesur Ghat, 95 miles below Hurdwar.

The surface at this point lies as follows :—

	Feet.	Inches.
Water at the Gurmukhtesur ghat, below zero at Myapoor	265	5·0
Surface of country at Futtigurh branch 45 miles	219	0·5
Surface main branch at Moradnuggur.........................	197	8·9

showing that the Ganges here lies 67 ft. 8·1 in. below the backbone or ridge of the watershed of the country at points parallel to each other.

The accompanying table exhibits very clearly the levels of the cross section in the line of country through which the Futtigurh branch runs. Many of these levels terminated on the top of the bank overlooking the Ganges; the following, however, were carried to the main river, and will show the fall of the surface of the river between the different points measured in a straight line:—

	Miles.		Fall. Feet.	Fall. Inches.
From Gurmukhtesur to near Anoopshuhur.	31	...	55	2·6
„ Anoopshuhur to Shoron	49½	...	64	4·9
„ Shoron to Puttiali	22	...	35	7·3
„ Puttiali to Futtigurh	47½	...	64	6·3
„ Futtigurh to Kumalgunj	8	...	6	0·9
„ Kumalgunj to 22 miles south	22	...	25	3·1

TABLE showing the Level of the Ganges, Futtigurh Branch, East Kali Nuddi, and Main Canal, relatively to each other.

No. of Miles from the Futtighur Branch Head, downwards on the Futtigurh Branch and on the Main Canal.	Levels showing Depression of Country below zero at Myapoor. Left, or Ganges. Ft.	In.	Centre or Futtigurh Branch. Ft.	In.	Right East Kali Nuddi. Ft.	In.	Extreme Right, Main Canal. Ft.	In.	—
5	142	6·7	134	3·7	...		125	4·8	
10	139	5·3	143	8·4	49	4·1	133	9·1	
15	160	11·3	154	5·1	66	7·0	141	6·2	
20	176	6·2	170	11·3	184	1·6	155	2 4	On top of bank of Ganges.
25	200	6·6	179	2·6	192	6·9	160	4·5	
30	200	2·9	197	1·5	204	7·2	163	6·9	
35	212	4·6	201	11·6	216	4·3	177	10·2	
40	221	11·8	208	8·7	226	11·4	185	7·4	
45	270	5·0	223	2·5	232	11·1	189	8·1	On Ganges River surface of water, low water.
50	231	4·4	228	5·1	253	3·2	199	8·5	On top of bank.
55	237	9·5	235	10·4	266	4·9	208	9·8	
60	280	11·6	248	2·4	280	7·3	216	8·6	On the Ganges River Bolundshuhur or East Kali Nuddi.
65	286	9·7	258	7·5	290	2·9	224	1·9	
70	296	8·8	266	11·3	297	10·9	227	9·5	On Ganges River, low water.
75	304	11·2	274	11·1	303	11·4	241	3 2	
80	320	8·1	286	4·9	309	6·9	248	8·0	On Ganges River Anoopshuhur on the Ganges, low water.

No. of Miles from the Futtighur Branch Head, downwards on the Futtigurh Branch and on the Main Canal.	Levels showing Depression of Country below zero at Myapoor.				—
	Left, or Ganges.	Centre or Futtigurh Branch.	Right, East Kali Nuddi.	Extreme Right, Main Canal.	
85	326 4·6	296 3·8	317 8·6	253 0·9	On Ganges River, low water.
90	334 2·5	303 8·4	322 4·7	258 9·6	
95	343 10·4	312 6·8	337 10·2	267 11·6	
100	346 11·2	321 10·6	347 11·7	271 0·3	
105	353 4·3	339 10·6	356 6·8	283 11·4	Old branch of Ganges, low water.
110	364 2·4	336 9·9	365 8·8	290 9·5	
115	367 0·7	342 3·1	372 6·2	300 1·0	
120	375 2·4	350 8·1	380 2·3	308 0·7	
125	385 0·5	353 6·1	388 4·5	314 3·7	
130	397 10·0	365 5·3	396 10·6	319 11·0	
135	406 2·4	372 6·2	397 4·1	330 0·7	
140	413 1·2	377 11·7	408 11·6	338 6·3	
145	420 7·8	383 3·8	416 3·0	341 10·8	
150	434 0·2	388 11·8	428 10·5	349 2·9	
155	438 0·2	395 0·1	430 3·6	356 4·9	
160	447 2·7	407 5·8	437 10·9	360 3·5	On Ganges River, low water.
165	451 2·4	409 10·7	446 1·9	366 2·5	
170	457 10·4	416 8·2	449 5·8	374 7·2	
175	467 10·4	422 9·2	457 7·0	379 6·0	
180	474 3·0	433 8·3	465 8·9	383 3·7	
185	480 6·0	436 2·7	472 8·2	387 10·5	Branch of Ganges, Furrukabad, near the Ganges, low water.
190	485 2·1	445 11·4	476 4·2	391 2·1	Ganges River, Futtigurh, low water.
195	491 3·0	451 4·0	488 0·3	398 8·4	Ganges River, Kumalgunj, low water.

Note.—By some oversight the figures in Plate VI. of the Atlas of the Ganges Canal Report, have not been reduced to the true zero at Myapoor. The flooring of the Futtigurh branch head being noted as 161 feet 7·8 inches, whereas, in the sheet of Proof Levels this is shown to be 133 feet 7·1 inches; a deduction of 28 feet 0·7 inches has to be made therefore from all the figures in Plate VI. to reduce them to the true zero of Myapoor.

Following the river in all its tortuosities, not only of course, but of winding in its own bed during the dry weather months, the above average, which is 1·39 feet per mile, or 251 feet 1·1 inches in 180 miles, would be very much reduced.

On the 8 miles between Futtigurh and Kumalgunj the fall, as above stated, is 9·1 inches per mile on the 150 miles preceding, viz., from Gurmukhtesur to Futtigurh, the average slope is 1·46 feet per mile, the total fall being 219 ft. 8·9 in.

Were we to determine the slopes of the surface-water of the Ganges from Gurmukhtesur to 22 miles south of Kumalgunj as varying from 1·25 to 0.75 foot per mile, we should not, I suspect, be very far wrong in our calculations.

From the above point on the Ganges, 22 miles below Kumalgunj to Cawnpoor, the distance is about 63 miles, and the surface of the river at the two extremes stands as follows with reference to the Myapoor zero—

	Feet.	Inches.
Ganges 22 inches below Kumalgunj	516	6·1
Ganges at locks at Cawnpoor agreeably to Captain G. Hutchinson's levels	566	4·0
Difference	49	9·9

or on the total distance 0·793 foot per mile. By the windings of the river this would be reduced, so that by fixing 0·75 foot or 9 inches per mile as the probable fall of surface, we shall not be much at fault.

From Cawnpoor to Allahabad the distance may be estimated at 138 miles, and my levels of 1845 show the following results :—

	Feet.	Inches.
Ganges surface of water at Cawnpoor, 13th Jan., 1844	559	2·5
Jumna at Allahabad near junction with the Ganges	672	8·1
Difference	113	5·6

or on the total distance 0·826 foot per mile. We may fairly also reduce this by the windings of the river to 0·75 foot or 9 inches per mile.

Commencing therefore at Sookurtal, with the hypothetical surface level as before alluded to, we have—

	Feet.	Inches.
High level at Sookurtal..................	179	6 below zero.
Level of surface at Gurmukhtesur......	265	5
Difference	85	11

which on a distance of 50 miles gives a fall of 1·72 feet per mile, or 0·47 feet more per mile than I have estimated as that from Badshahpoor; on a distance of 10 miles to Sookurtal. A mean between these may perhaps give an approximation to the truth, viz., 1·64 feet per mile, or say 18 inches per mile.

We have, therefore, the following table as deduced from what has gone before—

	Inches.
Slope of river from 10 miles above Sookurtal to Sookurtal...	18
" " Sookurtal to Gurmukhtesur	18
" " Gurmukhtesur to 60 miles south ...	15
" " " 60 miles south ...	12
60 miles south to 22 miles south of Kumalgunj	9
22 miles south of Kamalgunj to Cawnpoor..................	9
Cawnpoor to Allahabad	9

With the slopes of the surface of the river, and those of the surface of the land on the ridge of the watershed, and the table as given at page 60, I suppose nobody can doubt the possibility, with such a preponderance of fall on the high land, of making a cut from the river so as to meet the surface of the country at a lower part of its course; and as Sir Arthur Cotton says, that he requires nothing else to satisfy him that my projection of the canal head at Hurdwar is wrong — that he neither requires to look at the river nor any of the topographical features connected with it—that if the levels meet the high land properly, he considers that he possesses all the necessary data—I have, I hope, at the expense of some trouble, satisfied him on this point, although he would have found the whole or the greater part of the information which I have now given, in my report on the Ganges Canal, a copy of which was sent to him immediately after it came from the press.

I have dwelt with as much care and attention, as the

data at my disposal would admit, on the slopes of the surface of the water in the dry weather of the Ganges, as these are elements of much importance to the establishment of a dam on Sir Arthur Cotton's plan. We will now, however, look to the construction of the dam.

Dam across the Ganges at Sookurtal below the Junction of the Solani.—It is to be understood that the early projection of the Ganges Canal works is in the hands of Sir A. Cotton; that he selects a point near Sookurtal for the Head, and that he carries his canal thence to Newarri, a line which I showed in my pamphlet would, on his required slope of 3 inches per mile, deliver water on the surface and on the backbone of the country.

In the map which accompanies his rejoinder, this line is drawn from Sookurtal to Newarri, cutting at once through the bank. The line, as he has figured it, would pass close to the town and cantonments of Meerut; he must, therefore, submit to be guided by the regulations of our sanitary discipline, and vary the line either by holding to the north, by which he will keep in deep digging, or by passing south of Meerut plunge at once into interference with the drainage of the country.

The dam (I write under correction) is to be constructed with its waste-board ten feet above the dry weather surface of the Ganges, and the sill or flooring of the canal-head is to be on the same level as the waste-board of the dam.

With a slope of three inches per mile, and with a head water maintained on the crest of the Dam, say 5 feet in height, it will be necessary, in order to secure a stream running into the canal at the rate of 1½ miles an hour and 5 feet in depth, to excavate a channel between 900 and 1,000[1] feet in width; and as the line of canal will not be allowed to run within 5 miles of the boundaries of the town and cantonments of Meerut, this width through deep digging will have to be continued for many miles, more or less interfered with by drainage, depending on whether the direction lies to the east or west of the town.[2]

The *danda* or high bank above Bhokurheeri is by no means unlike that which I have before described as existing in the neighbourhood of Etawah on the Jumna. It is a series of entangled and exaggerated ravines from 80 to 120 feet above the valley below.

On turning the corner towards Sookurtal, the character of this high bank is somewhat modified; it maintains a height varying from 70 feet or upwards to 40 or 45, but its raviny character is less marked. Its crest is surmounted by sand-hills, which continue to a considerable distance south. On the section which I crossed in taking a line of levels from Badshahpoor to Kumbhera, the high bank was composed of a substratum of sand with tabular masses of Kunkur at detached points, and above this Kunkur, sand, with a superincumbent stratum of good soil; upon this good soil was sand varying in depth, and depending very much on the extent of the sand-hills and drift for which that part of the country is notorious. The section above given is that of the whole line of bank, whether above or below

[1] A channel with a mean breadth of 950 feet, and depth 5 feet, with a slope of 3 inches per mile, will carry 6,700 cubic feet of water per second, with a mean velocity of a little less than $1\frac{1}{2}$ feet per second.

[2] The cantonments of Kurnal, formerly held to be one of the healthiest stations of the Bengal army, lying on the Western Jumna Canal, were removed to Umballa at a sacrifice to the Government of about three quarters of a million sterling, on account of its supposed unhealthy position, reputed to have been caused by canal inundation.

Sookurtal. It is that at Sookurtal itself, and it would, on the line marked by Sir Arthur Cotton, give him sand as the bed of his canal from the point where he leaves the low land or k'hadir onwards.

To proceed with the dam across the Ganges. This work would, in all probability, be not less than a mile or a mile and half in length ; it would, with the permanent elevation of the dam and its regulating apparatus (hardly removable in time for floods), be at least 15 feet above the dry weather surface of the river. The flanks of this work both on its masonry and earthen portions, would of course have to be raised in a degree corresponding with the calculated height of flood water, and both flanks would have to be protected against the inroads of whirlpools and violent action, which invariably accompany the passage of floods in these rivers.

The mouth of the canal, would have to be protected by masonry, stonework, or very extensive piling. What the depth of foundation would be, I know not ; but I am quite satisfied that Colonel Baird Smith is right in saying that if constructed similarly to those in Southern India, "they would inevitably fail on the first serious trial." (Baird Smith's *Cauveri, Kistna,* and *Godaveri,* p. 114. Smith, Elder and Co., 1856.)

We have, then, as far as I can understand, a dam whose wasteboard is raised 10 feet above the dry weather surface of the river, with an additional elevation of 5 feet for canal supply ; these 15 feet being flanked by embankments protected by stone or masonry of at least 5 feet in addition, or say 20 feet in total height from the dry weather surface of the river.

My argument is this—and it is formed (whatever Sir Arthur Cotton may say to the contrary) on long experience in dealing with rivers in the North-Western Provinces—that the tendency of the river at all times when subjected to being interfered with by dams, especially in floods, is to undermine the foundation *in front;* it is most markedly active in the flanks, which it endeavours to turn by every means in its power. I recollect at a point on the river just below the Gurmukhtesur Ghat, in the month of April, 1845, and, therefore, not in the monsoon, after a tremendous north-wester, when the river was running like a sea, passing a whirlpool which had established itself on the right bank, and was tearing away everything before it. I do not think that any masonry works or piling could have withstood the action of such water as I saw on that occasion.

In addition to the above, we have during floods, trees (whole *bur* or *banyan* trees, for instance) torn up by the roots, and rafts of portentous dimensions swept down the course of the river. For all this species of material a dam would afford the most perfect trap. Its crest would become an *entrepôt* for all the rubbish brought down from the mountains, and from the forests lying at their foot.

At the Nyashur dam on the Eastern Jumna Canal works, the centre of which used, in my day, to be opened out to within 2 feet of the flooring, or bed of the river, by sluices, I have seen a whole tree, as above described, after rolling along with the flood with frightful rapidity, settle itself on the dam. This was followed by others, branches, reeds, grass, &c., until the mass became top-heavy, when away it went, causing more or less injury to the dam.

For a work or board of works, as above described, including dam, embankments, regulating head, masonry and other works in the k'hadir below it, and excavation with bridges and drainage works, what would be a fair estimate? Sir Arthur Cotton says 75,000*l*.

My belief is that the estimate would exceed in

amount that for all my works from Hurdwar to Newarri. I should be very sorry to submit an estimate, being answerable that the same should not be exceeded, and being personally and pecuniarily responsible for all risk of failure and repairs during construction, for less than that sum.

I have before alluded to the perennial body of water that passes down the river, which at Sookurtal is more than 8,000 cubic feet a second in the dry months; I have also drawn attention to the periodical rains, and the irregular periods at which floods come down the river, leaving but a few months unaccompanied by action or increase to its waters. In addition to these elements of difficulty, there is an absence of building material at Sookurtal which would render the construction of a work like that proposed by Sir A. Cotton exceedingly costly.

Evils of Inundation.—Having constructed this dam and put it in operation, we now have to look at its effects on the country lying immediately above it. There is, say a permanent headwater maintained for the canal supply raised to a height of 15 feet above the low-water level; a maximum headwater in floods equal to 18 feet: supposing the slope of the bed of the river to be 1½ feet per mile[1] on its approach to the dam, a backwater would be given extending 10 and 12 miles respectively up the bed of the river, or looking at the Atlas of India (sheet 48) to a point as far back as Badshahpoor and its neighbourhood. The inundation caused by this backwater would in its more northern parts extend irregularly over a width of 13 miles, and

[1] Whether the slope is 1½ or 4 feet per mile, or whether the dam is 1 or 4 miles wide, the evil arising from the inundations would be merely one of degree. The same may be said whether the inundation is only 1 square mile or 100 square miles in extent.

would cover a superficial area of 80 square miles; I believe very much more, as this hardly includes the low lands that would come under the influence of inundations on the east or left side of the Ganges. To contract the area of inundation by embankments would be a work of not only enormous expense, but of very doubtful stability.

Destruction to cultivated Lands and Villages.—Malaria. —I am unable to say to what extent cultivated land would be submerged by the above arrangement, it would, however, be great; villages, and their sites would also in all probability suffer; but it is not difficult to understand the effects upon the country caused by the introduction of a lake with its attendant morasses, of either this size or one of one-tenth its dimensions. It would be a great centre of malaria, and a harbour for wild beasts, which are already in quite sufficient abundance in the neighbourhood. We should, in fact, under the plea of benefiting the country by irrigation works, introduce an evil of the greatest magnitude and one that would be a curse upon the country. No Government would hear with patience of such a design, and had I at the time when the canal works were projected—viz., previous to the famine in 1838—proposed to introduce upon the face of the Northern Doab a canal with such a deformity as its leading feature, I should have been very properly laughed at, and the project which had given me so much thought and labour, would have fallen to the ground.

The fact is that Sir Arthur Cotton with his Madras experience looks upon sanitary interference as totally uncalled for, and Medical Committees he treats with all the respect conferred upon them in his report to the East India Irrigation Company: whether the climate of Madras, however, is capable of being independent of regulations on this subject or not, that of the North-West is most assuredly not independent of them, and the canal department has very stringent rules by which it is limited in all its operations. I recollect when the late Colonel Baird Smith joined me on his return from his inspection of the irrigation works in Madras, he mentioned that what struck him most, in a general way, was the extraordinary indifference not only of the engineers, but apparently of the Madras Government, to sanitary discipline, in the first place, and to the accommodation of the country in means for crossing the canals, in the second. He alluded to the liability to accidents of a most serious nature from breaches in heavy floods, or even floods of no great importance, arising from the permanent elevation given to the beds of the great rivers above the dams; to the indifference about the alignments of the canals; to the restriction of the water to its proper channel; in fact, to the absence of all the expensive care that we in the North-West are called upon to give to matters of this sort. On the subject of accommodation, there was an absence of bridges that was marvellous in the eyes of an engineer from the North-West; he mentioned that miles may be traversed without a bridge being met with, ferry-boats being the usual method of giving accommodation to the cultivators. That, in fact, the normal way of passing the canals was by ferry-boats, and that frequently villages were cut off from their village lands.

Now, bridges are very expensive, and when, as in the North-Western Provinces, we are made to build them at every three miles, or even less, should such be necessary for the accommodation of the people, their cost adds largely to the estimate; when, moreover, these bridges are made with an elevation of arch sufficient to pass large boats, or if fitted with moveable apparatus for the same purpose, they become still more expensive, and still

6—2

further add to the general estimate. The device, therefore, of having *no bridges at all*, or as few bridges as possible, is an ingenious as well as an economical one, but it must be a cause of extreme inconvenience to the country; and to the cultivators, a very great hardship.

At any rate we cannot in the North-Western Provinces overlook sanitary discipline: the rifeness of vegetation is such, on land flooded by the canals, or in channels with low slopes, and with bodies of water flowing with small depths, that water-plants, reeds, and grass spring up in an incalculably short period of time, so as in one case to be a nuisance to the neighbourhood, and in the other to be a positive detriment to the flow of the water—they are, in fact, nuisances in the full signification of the term—precisely as Sir Arthur Cotton's dams would be nuisances to be avoided, as public enemies to the salubrity of the country.

At page 104 of Sir A. Cotton's pamphlet, he prints an extract from the late Colonel Baird Smith's Famine Report, as proving that the Ganges and Jumna had not been *properly examined* [1] below the Solani. The extract is only a *portion* of a paragraph, a very material part, as bearing on my views, and clearly on those of the writer, having been omitted. I give the paragraph 123 *in extenso;* (it will be observed that Sir A. Cotton, in his rejoinder, p. 104, commences his extract from the words, "From 50 to 70 feet.") "The Ganges and Jumna "only can be rightly termed irrigation rivers, and they

[1] The expression "properly examined" is not very precise: Colonel Baird Smith's views were clearly based on a much wider principle than those of mere engineering. I examined the bed of the river as far south as the Gurmukhtesur Ghat, to see whether there was any likely spot for a permanent head, but I confess with as little idea of attempting to lift the water by a dam across the river on Sir Arthur Cotton's or any other plan, as of lifting the supply by machinery.

" only will ever exercise any very important influence on " the security of the districts lying between them. So " rapidly, however, do both these rivers bury themselves " in deep valleys, that their waters early cease to be " available for irrigation after they have left the near " neighbourhood of the Mountains. *Their valleys, too, are " of such extent, and in many localities so densely populated, " and so well cultivated, that such Works as would raise the " surface water on the Doab are almost shut out from con- " sideration, by reason of the destruction to property which " they would cause.* From 50 to 70 feet represent the " general depth of the great rivers beneath the surface " level of the country, and from 1½ to 6 miles represent " the width of the troughs or valleys in which they flow. " Under these conditions the prospects of making more " of these rivers than has already been made is not " encouraging. At the same time the question," (*i. e.* the whole question) " has never been systematically examined. " The information available is fragmentary and incom- " plete. Using it as well as I could, I have come to the " conclusion at present, that no works directed to the de- " livery of water on the high lands of the Doab from " any points on the Ganges or Jumna, more than 12 or " 15 miles below their respective places of departure " from the Mountains, are likely to be financially practi- " cable. Physically practicable of course they are, but " Dams of such magnitude would be required across the " Rivers, and Channels of such depths through the high " lands, that the cost would counterbalance the gain so " greatly, that it would probably be idle to think of " executing them. But I would gladly see the matter " submitted to intelligent examination, as it may be that " the imperfection of our present knowledge has led to " narrower views being taken on the question than are " right. Beyond inquiry of this kind, however, it

" would not be prudent to carry my present recommen-
" dations."

The italics in the above are mine. Had I been writing on the subject of this famine, under the same pressure, and with the same interesting objects before me, there is not one word in the above passage that I would have omitted. Famine was on the land, and every measure had to be considered, and well considered, to prevent as far as possible a recurrence of it. The meaning of Colonel Baird Smith must be misinterpreted, I imagine, if he is supposed to limit his inquiries to the mere engineering difficulty of building a dam; he especially alludes to other equally important points: destruction of property, and the effects of inundation. The observation that "the question has never been systematically ex-" amined," I apprehend is directed to the general question, and not to that of the dam only. There were difficulties on all hands, and his object was to have a commission of inquiry, to discover not merely whether a dam *could* be constructed across the k'hadir of the river, but to see to what extent works of this sort would affect the *public revenue, private interests*, and the *salubrity of the country*. Colonel Baird Smith's paragraph bears in my mind a very different interpretation from that which Sir A. Cotton places on it. Referring again to an extract from Colonel Baird Smith's famine Report, par. 37, on the use of the Sutlej, Sir A. Cotton remarks at page 106 of his pamphlet,—" Further on in the report I last referred to,
" in speaking of the Sutlej river, Colonel B. Smith pro-
" poses this very plan of drawing off its water *at points*
" *far from the hills*. He says, 'It is not at all necessary
" 'to suppose that a canal from the Sutlej, at a high
" 'level, will exhaust the capabilities of that river for
" 'agricultural purposes. Such a canal would be the
" 'first and best use of the waters, but hereafter it may

" 'be both expedient and practicable to draw other lines " 'from lower levels, which, *though not efficient, nor so* " '*reliable* in their action, may still become very valuable, " 'and give additional guarantee for the security of that " 'tract.' "

In penning the words which I have italicized in the above extract from Col. B. Smith's paper, I do not believe that he ever thought of anicuts or dams across the river; he was manifestly alluding to cuts made from the sides *at low levels*, as *has been* done, and *is* done at certain seasons of the year constantly.[1] The wonder expressed by Sir Arthur Cotton that after having seen the Madras works, Col. B. Smith should write of "dams of such magnitude, and channels of such depth "through the land," is quite characteristic. To my mind, it shows distinctly that Col. Baird Smith placed the true value upon the comparative difficulties of the canal works on the Madras Deltas and those which he refers to in the troughs of the great rivers in the North-west. Sir A. Cotton writes (see p. 119 of his pamphlet), when referring to me: "He thinks that I had not sufficient data for that opinion. I reply that I only wanted "one piece of information, which was the height of the "country above the river, and this by no means to any

[1] In par. 141 of the same report, Colonel Baird Smith writes—"I "have a strong impression, though it is unsupported by any levels, that "the Ganges might be turned to account for the irrigation of part of the "Bijnore district. I would be glad to hear of the practicability of "this being determined by actual survey. About 1,000 cubic feet per "second thrown into that district would almost secure it against future "injury from drought; and if the levels proved favourable from some "point considerably below the Ganges Canal heads, such a supply "might be available in all years, as the percolation through the boulder "bed of the river is always great." Can it be supposed that Colonel Baird Smith contemplated a dam or anicut across the Ganges, for the supply of 1,000 cubic feet per second?

" great nicety, *for it was not a question of whether the* " *proposed new head canal must be* 10 *miles or* 50 *long.* " This information I got from one of the local officers, " and no doubt it was quite correct. It referred to the " Futigurh branch. As to the *practicability* of building " a weir, of course I did not require any detailed infor- " mation on that: I saw the Ganges in many places, and " found that it was *just of the same character as our weirs,* " and I know, of course, *that what had been done in* " *Madras in many places, could be done here.*"

The fact is, if everything is to be taken " of course," and if neither the breadth of the k'hadir, nor the slope of the river, nor any of the hydrographical details, are worthy of consideration, an engineer may jump to any conclusion. Although indifferent to the width of the k'hadir, and consequently to the length of the dam and its embankments, Sir A. Cotton somewhat inconsistently determines the cost of the work, and gives an estimate thereof without any hesitation. At page 105, when criticizing Col. Baird Smith's objections, he proceeds: " He himself" (Col. Baird Smith) " had seen the dams " across the Godaveri, Kistna, and Coleroon, the smallest " of them larger than one would be at the mouth of the " Solani, and the largest of them across a river of eight " times the width and about six times the volume of the " Ganges there."—Page 105, Sir A. Cotton's pamphlet.

Eight times the width of the Ganges, viz., at Sookertal! [1]

[1] Now I find by reference to Col. Baird Smith's reports, and others, that the width of these three great rivers at the point where the dams are built, are as follows:—

Cauveri, 1 mile, or thereabouts (B. Smith's map).

Kistna, $1\frac{3}{4}$ to $2\frac{3}{4}$ miles wide (B. Smith).

Godaveri, "2,000 yards immediately above, and 6,000 yards *at* the " dam, or nearly $3\frac{1}{2}$ miles, 1,000 or 1,500 yards being occupied by " islands" (Baird Smith); the actual width in miles being, without

Whence does he derive his information? Col. Baird Smith wrote of works that he had seen, and having seen them did not hesitate to give an opinion upon them. Sir Arthur Cotton, on the contrary, who not only has not seen the Ganges at the point where the Solani joins it, but declares that for his purpose there is no necessity to see it, does not hesitate apparently to draw a comparison between its *width* at that point and that of the Madras rivers.

I hold that when Sir Arthur Cotton constitutes himself monitor and censor-general of my operations, he ought to be cautious in what he asserts, at any rate in the cardinal matter of figures. The propriety of avoiding statements, not borne out by facts, might also be worthy of his consideration.

Sir A. Cotton has, in his original report to the East India Irrigation Company, declared that I had, in projecting the head of the Ganges Canal above Hurdwar, by unnecessarily excavating many miles of canal and projecting most expensive masonry works, in connection with the mountain torrents and the k'hadir, put the Government to an expense of 75 laks of rupees, *when he could have gained the same object at* $\frac{1}{10}$*th of the above cost, or for* 7½ *laks of rupees, by simply constructing a dam on the Ganges below the junction of the Solani, and excavating a canal from it of only* 12 *miles in length.*[1] After having deliberately

---

the islands, either 2 miles and 5 furlongs or 2 miles and a little more than 7 furlongs.

In the *Edinburgh Review*, January, 1854, it is stated to be 2 miles wide, divided by islands into four channels.

[1] *See* p. 49 of "Reply to Statements:" Sir Arthur Cotton writes,—"In the first place, as the head of the canal from Hurdwar to Roorkee, "20 miles, which has so great a fall, and crosses all the heavy drainage "of the sub-Himalayas, has cost about ¾ of a million sterling, it is "impossible that it could have been more expensive than that to have

brought an accusation to this effect against me, by a specific statement professedly borne out by the above figures, Sir A. Cotton quietly drops the figures, and in the map which is the frontispiece to his rejoinder, takes possession of an hypothetical line between Sookertal and Newarri:—two places which, in p. 8 of my reply to his statements, I showed to be the extremes of a line that would be adapted to the levels of a canal on a slope of three inches per mile, and separated from each other in a straight line of *not* 12, *but* 51 *miles*. He states in his rejoinder that it was not a question whether it was to be 10 or 50 miles, and that *distance*, therefore, was *immaterial*. It may be *immaterial* to the mere possibility of cutting a canal so that the levels may meet the surface of the high land of the Doab, a possibility that nobody ever doubted; but it is not so to his charge against me. Recklessness of accusation of this sort cannot be passed over in silence. In my reply to General Cotton's statements made in his so-called Private Memorandum to the East India Irrigation Company, with a temper that I now look back upon with astonishment, I answered each charge, and I frankly admitted the

" thrown a weir across the Ganges below the confluence of the Solani, " and cut the head of the canal from there. But further I was informed " by an officer of the canal department, that he had taken the level " from the Futtigurh branch of the canal, to the neighbouring bed of " the Ganges in two places, and found it 40 feet in each, while the fall " of the country there is about 3 feet a mile. Hence if the water of " the river were raised 10 feet by a weir, and the head of the canal " cut from it with a fall of half a foot a mile, gaining 2½ feet a mile " upon the slope of the country, it would only require a cut of 12 miles " in length to lead the water out upon the present level of the canal, " which could not possibly be an expensive work; it could not certainly " cost more than $\frac{1}{10}$th of that of the present head of the canal above that " point, while including also the permanent weir which the present " head of the channel has not."

error of having given an excess of slope, thereby causing a velocity to the stream that had been injurious to the works and obstructive to irrigation; an error which from the first had been recognized, and with the discovery of which Sir Arthur Cotton had nothing whatever to do. An acknowledgment of this error might have satisfied my greatest enemy. Sir Arthur Cotton, however, is not so satisfied, and he replies in a tone of such assumption, that the rejoinder is, perhaps, more offensive than his original paper was depreciatory. The following extract, however, from Colonel Baird Smith's report on the irrigation works at Madras will show, that Sir Arthur Cotton does not confine his recklessness to myself, or to other individuals, but that he has a peculiar notion of morality in his dealings with the Government. In referring to the increased expenditure over estimates submitted by General Cotton for the Coleroon works, Colonel Baird Smith writes:—"To frame estimates so that they shall "represent, as nearly as all the knowledge at command "permits, the liabilities of the Government in under-"taking the works, is an engineer officer's clear and "unquestionable duty. I think that great evils must "ultimately result from any tampering with its principle, "and as most unfortunately the original estimates for the "Coleroon works were, as subsequently avowed, made de-"signedly lower than they ought to have been, with a view "to inducing Government to commit itself to the works, "I am not surprised that confidence in their Projector "should be somewhat impaired, so far at any rate as "probable expense is concerned."—(*See* p. 32, *Cauveri, Kistna, and Godaveri.*) This having been the case, I need be in no astonishment at the way in which I have been dealt with; or be in any doubt as to the value of his estimates!

Not contented with the line above noted, which, as I have in a former part of this paper shown, would require a considerable detour to prevent it from interfering with the town and cantonments of Meerut, he has on his frontispiece map traced another from the Ganges at Anoopshuhur to the main canal at a point just above the separation of the Cawnpoor and Etawah terminals, connecting it with a proposed branch extending between the Eesun and the East Kalli Nuddi.

This new hypothetical line being drawn parallel, or nearly so, to that between Sookurtal and Newarri would, as a fair piece of guess-work, be similarly circumstanced as to levels. Nor has Sir Arthur Cotton been far wrong. I find that the following are the relative levels from the zero at Myapoor:—

	Feet.	Inches.
Level of surface of water of the Ganges River above Anoopshuhur	320	8·1
Level of surface of country at Nanoon, or the point of separation between the Cawnpoor and Etawah terminals	318	7·1

Supposing, therefore, that the waste-board of his dam is raised 10 or 15 feet above the surface of the Ganges, and that a slope of 6 inches per mile (which is the least that could be given to a canal feeder in such a position) is allowed, this cut or feeder would meet the surface of the high land at points 3 and 6 miles respectively below the separation of the two terminals. The guess here, therefore, has been more successful than on the former occasion; but guesses are not always to be depended upon.

Look at his estimate for completing the Ganges Canal project, which he submitted to the E. I. Irrigation Company! Is this a matter of guess-work and to be treated lightly? an estimate which no doubt led the Company to offer to purchase the canal for 1½ millions? Is this to be considered a serious matter or not? (*See* p. 64 of my "Reply to Statements.")

	£
"Additional heads with weir on the Ganges and "Jumna 200 or 300 miles below the Solani ...	200,000"

That is to say, on the Jumna, 1 head not far below Agra; or 1 head near Kalpi and above the junction of the Betwa.

On the Ganges, 1 head below Futtigurh; or 1 head near Futtipoor, and not 100 miles from Allahabad.

And the Company is gravely told that these works (dams, canals, and all,) will only cost 200,000*l*., or 20 laks of rupees!

In p. 105 of his pamphlet, he proceeds in a manner that I seriously deprecate. In my reply to Sir A. Cotton's strictures I avoided, to the best of my ability, and certainly with the best intentions, any attempt at drawing comparisons between the canal works in Madras and those of the North-Western Provinces; at elevating our works by detracting from theirs; by assertions that they were more difficult with us than with them; or that, in fact, we, as engineers, were at all cleverer than they were. On that occasion, however, Sir A. Cotton forced the Gunnarum aqueduct upon me, as a work that might have been taken as a pattern for my aqueduct over the Solani. He now brings into, what he considers, a favourable contrast, the works of the Madras Irrigation Company, of which he writes as follows, p. 105 of his pamphlet:—

"Compare the work now advocated,"[1] writes Sir A. Cotton, "with what is now nearly accomplished by the

[1] I understand this to mean his proposed dam and cut from the Ganges below the junction of the Solani; the asserted extravagant expenditure on my project having been pointed out in a previous paragraph.

" Madras Irrigation Company on the Toombuddra river " at Kurnool; which river is there about 150[1] feet below " the water-shed, immediately south of the confluence of " the Toombuddra and Kistna. The company have con- " structed an anicut, or weir, more than 1¼ miles in " length across the river, and they have also nearly " completed a canal to carry 400,000 cubic yards per " hour (3,200 cubic feet per second) for 72 miles through " a very difficult rocky and undulating country, including " a stone aqueduct across the Hindri river of 300 yards' " length, crossing also several small streams, besides a " considerable rocky cutting through the watershed " itself; and the whole of this will have cost, I believe, " 200,000*l*., or say, 250,000*l*."

Why should the Madras Irrigation Company be dragged into this discussion except with a view to glorify an undertaking projected under the auspices of Sir Arthur Cotton? The readers of the pamphlet will necessarily accept a statement of this sort coming from such high authority, and would not suppose that there could be any doubt in its correctness. The facts are these:—

Up to April, 1863, nearly 36 laks of rupees, that is to say, 360,000*l*. sterling, had been expended on the above works, the state of which in the month of August, four months later, was as follows:—

Anicut at the Soonkasala Head incomplete, with a breach in it of 80 or 100 feet in width, which the engineers were about to attempt to close. On this work nearly double the amount of estimate had been expended, and it was yet incomplete. The Hindri aqueduct in-

[1] This will deceive no one who understands the position and structure of the high bank of the Ganges, and that of the Mittacondal cutting, the point referred to, south of the confluence of the Toombuddra and Kistna.

complete, and all the money of the estimate spent. The excavation of 72 miles exceedingly incomplete; no bridges built, and, in fact, very few bridges had been estimated for. On 17 miles between the Soonkasala Head and the Hindri aqueduct there were no bridges. The embankments were imperfect and unconsolidated, and great damage had been caused by breaches during heavy rains. Many miles of the canal have been constructed intentionally and for economy's sake, *without any embankments at all on its right, the water being allowed to find its own level by inundation over the surface of the country:* not much, I should say, to the benefit of the people, in a sanitary point of view.

With this statement, or a statement to this effect, before the Company, Sir Arthur Cotton has no hesitation in making his pamphlet an advertisement for giving a colour to the progress of the works which really does not exist; the whole being a mere hallucination, convenient to his argument, as drawing a comparison favourable to engineering works under Madras supervision.

From what I have shown as to the relative levels of the surface of the country and of the Ganges in its passage to Allahabad, it will be distinctly seen that the further we proceed down the course of the river, the less is the difference of slope, so that a dam constructed (if such were advisable or of the slightest use,) 300 miles below the Solani, could not be excavated under the same advantages of fall in country's surface as it would be in the higher regions. The evils that would attend on the construction of the dam itself would be much greater, arising from increased extent of back water, with waste-board raised 15 feet instead of 10, as proposed for the Sookurtal work. The k'hadir also becomes more studded with villages in its lower than in its higher regions.

From registers kept at Futtigurh and Cawnpoor, to which I have referred in a former part of this paper, the rise of flood during rains at the former place is on an average of 11 years equal to 9 feet 3 inches, at the latter 12 feet 8 inches; so that a dam raised 15 feet with flood water on the top of it, would cause an elevation to the surface of the water which would not only inundate the k'hadir at any point on its whole width, but extend in many places far inland. The reduction in depth of water at the crest of the dam, on its approach to the work, would not materially affect the above calculation.

Having thus gone, at greater length than I ever intended, into the subject of these canal heads, I will now, as promised in the early part of this paper, give a summary of what I consider to be the objections to Sir Arthur Cotton's dams, especially that one below the mouth of the Solani.

1st. Engineering difficulties of making and maintaining a permanent dam across the Ganges on Sir A. Cotton's plan.

i. Bed confined in a trough, and of a sandy and treacherous character.

ii. Volume of perennial supply in the river.

iii. Limited period during which the river is left untouched by floods; uncertainty of period and dangerous nature of these floods.

iv. Absence of stone and lime quarries, and scarcity of brick, earth, and other material.

v. Rafts, trees, and rubbish floated down during floods.

2nd. Effects upon villages and valuable lands by backwater and inundation.

i. A great portion of the low land on the k'hadir is rich in villages, and notorious for the value of its produce; a rise of the surface of the Ganges of 20 feet or even of 15 would lead to the destruction of many that came under the influence of the inundation. There are points in the Jumna where the damage would be more severe than on the Ganges. I believe that a rise of 30 feet would flood any k'hadir land on either of the rivers.

3rd. Evils in a sanitary point of view.

i. I have before explained the probable effect upon the k'hadir of a dam, with its waste-board raised 10 feet above the low-water level of the river, at Sookurtal, at a point where the slope of the river is much greater than it is in the lower part of its course. I have shown with the data upon which I have gone, that this dam would during the rains produce a lake extending over a surface of 80 square miles.

On dams placed lower down the course of the river the evils would be, in all probability, greater.

As Sir Arthur Cotton considers inspection of site as unnecessary, he must, "*of course*" (using his own language), know nothing about the evils that an inundation of this sort would produce. The Jogipoor jheel or marsh, which lies in the neighbourhood of Sookurtal, and would come under the influence of this inundation, is, without any artificial inundation at all, one of the most notorious spots in the district for wild animals. But what is this in comparison to Sir Arthur Cotton's projected lake—or lakes rather?—for both the Ganges and Jumna are to be provided with them at various spots on their course.

ii. What would be the effect of introducing these inundations and marshes on the face of the country? This I leave to the faculty and to sanitary commissions, keeping in mind the known injurious results and costly experience gained at Kurnal by the loss to the Government of nearly three-quarters of a million sterling invested in cantonments compulsorily abandoned.

What with miasma, and its concomitant fevers—what with wild beasts, and their predatory habits—it requires the introduction of new blood, in the shape of a Madras engineer of the high position in which Sir Arthur Cotton is, to propose and seriously to recommend the establishment of such evils.

What the feelings of the present Government may be on matters of sanitary discipline I know not; but I can assert without fear of contradiction that had I at any time, previously to my departure from India in 1854, proposed works like those now advocated by Sir A. Cotton, they would have been scouted. Even the elevation of the waters of the Hindun and West Kalli Nuddi, which at page 39 of my "Reply to Statements" I refer to as the only available means of obtaining an additional supply of water for the Ganges Canal in its whole course from Hurdwar to its lower terminus, and which would do comparatively little injury in the destruction of villages and land, was, at the time of its being proposed by Captain Debude in 1831, or thereabouts, looked upon with dismay on account of its effects on the health of the country. At the present period it would, I suspect, be fatal to the projection of the above works (small as their basins would be), quite independently of any question on their engineering difficulties.

One word in conclusion. In my pamphlet in reply to Sir Arthur Cotton's so-called *Private Memorandum*, although written for a public company which used it, with Sir Arthur Cotton's cognizance, as a damaging public document, in order to depreciate, in the eyes of the Government, the property for which they were bidding, I was especially careful that no remark should be made by me on any statement in Sir Arthur Cotton's paper without a foot-note referring to the page in which that statement was made. The object of this arrangement was to restrict the discussion within certain limits.

I confess my surprise, therefore, at finding that in the copy of this pamphlet which Sir Arthur Cotton has reprinted with his rejoinder, all these notes of reference have been suppressed. The text, moreover, has been italicized in a way that I cannot be responsible for.

Feb. 23, 1864.

APPENDIX.

EXTRACT *from* "A REPLY *to Statements made by Major-General Sir Arthur Cotton on the Projection of the Ganges Canal Works*," p. 12.

Fundamental mistake No. 3 stands as follows:—

"'3. The whole of the masonry are works of brick, while the most "'suitable stone for hydraulic works is procurable in the Sub-Hima- "'layas: this is a most inexplicable mistake.'" In another part of "the paper, Sir A. Cotton writes: 'the excellent stone of Hurdwar;'[1] "and in commencing his strictures, observes—'There is nothing "'more inexplicable than this in the whole matter. I cannot find a "'word of discussion on this point in the published reports on the "'project.'[2]

"The strictures convey a sweeping condemnation on brick masonry "to which I by no means agree; nevertheless, where good stone is to "be procured at a reasonable price, no man in his senses would select "brick. The Sewalik sandstone, however, is of very uncertain quality, "and is attended by beds of conglomerate of a similar character. It "varies from extreme friability to a crystalline[3] rock; in all the grada- "tions through which it passes it is to be worked without any great "difficulty. The unequal quality of the stone, however, and the pre- "ponderance of that of a very inferior order, renders it a somewhat "dangerous material to be introduced on public works. The town of "Hurdwar and Kunkhul, the ruins of Badshahmuhal on the Jumna, "those on the left of the Ganges, and numerous tombs and mosques in "the vicinity of the hills, are built with this stone. The stone that is "used is procured at considerable expense and with great difficulty; "hard portions are selected at distant and detached points out of "*masses* of the softer rock, and brought to Hurdwar and Kunkhul for

[1] Page 52. [2] Page 47. [3] Vide explanation, supra, p. 14.

"the use of the stonecutters. As a rule, however, the Sewalik sand-"stone is notoriously inferior as a material for building. Stone of the "quality that I should have selected (some of which has been used in "the Myapoor Regulating Bridge) was much too expensive; and as "my estimate of brick masonry is of a more sanguine nature than "that of Sir A. Cotton, the heavy expense that the use of good Sewalik "stone for the masonry, or even for the floorings and walls of the falls "and locks, would have entailed upon the works, determined me on the "use of brick.

"With reference to the above, I may quote paragraph No. 70 of "Colonel Turnbull's Report on the Permanent Head-works Ganges "Canal, November, 1862. Colonel Turnbull writes:—'Some time "'before Colonel Rundall's visit to the head-works, Mr. Login was "'directed to explore the neighbouring hills at Hurdwar, for the very "'hard, heavy conglomerate adverted to in his report: and having "'done so, in company with the professor of geology in the Civil "'Engineering College of Roorkee, Mr. H. B. Medlicott, he ascertained "'that such stone is only to be found in detached masses along the "'hill-side, or in irregular deposits, where it lies in its bed, and that "'the rock adjoining it was quite unfitted for the proposed work "'nearer than ten miles from its site. That the gradient for a tramway "'to connect the works with the hills would be 1 in 13 feet, and that, "'therefore, quarried stone of 3 to 5 tons weight, as proposed by "'Colonel Rundall, could not be placed upon the works at less than "'8 annas per foot.'

"From what I hear, the reason why brick masonry has failed in "the falls (or weirs, as designated by Sir A. Cotton) is, that a pressure "of water has been brought to bear upon the floorings of a nature far "beyond what I contemplated; and I have the best authority for "asserting that even in these cases the general character of the brick-"work has been proof against the most exaggerated action of the "water. Failure has been attendant on badly-constructed work. I "am quite willing to agree with Sir A. Cotton that stone is better than "brick, as a general rule, but I would prefer good brick to stone of "doubtful quality.

"Sir A. Cotton is mistaken in supposing that the boulders (or "pebbles to which he refers [1]) found in the bed of the Ganges and its "tributaries have met with the fate that he bewails for the sandstone. "I have always been a great advocate for the use of this material, "having had before my eyes the gigantic ruins of Badshahmuhal, and

[1] Page 48.